THE LAST SLAVE TRADERS

Pierre Meunier

Spectrum Books Limited
Ibadan
Benin City • Kaduna • Lagos • Owerri

Published by
Spectrum Books Limited
Spectrum House
Ring Road
PMB 5612
Ibadan, Nigeria

in association with
Safari Books (Export) Limited
1st Floor
17 Bond Street
St Helier
Jersey JE2 3NP
Channel Islands
United Kingdom

Europe and USA Distributor
African Books Collective Ltd
The Jam Factory
27 Park End Street
Oxford OX1, 1HU, UK

© Pierre Meunier

First Published 1999

All rights reserved. This book is copyright and so no part of it may be reproduced, stored in a retrieval system, or transmitted, in any form or by any means, electronic, mechanical, electrostatic, magnetic tape, photocopying, or otherwise, without the prior written permission of the copyright owner.

ISBN 978–029–070–2

Printed by Polygraphics Venture Limited Ibadan

CHARACTERS

JADIN:	Managing Director of OSCA, a West African Trading Company — an expatriate.
GRANIER:	Deputy Director - an expatriate.
THE NEW MAN:	A newly employed person whom Jadin simply refers to as "the new man", rather than by his name - an expatriate.
THE POET:	An expatriate.
THE HUNTER:	An expatriate.
A LOCAL POLICEMAN	
THE PAINTER:	An expatriate
THE SPORTSMAN:	An expatriate
THE PLAYBOY:	An expatriate
ALEXANDER:	The old cook in OSCA's canteen
SUNDAY:	An indigene working with OSCA.
THE YOUNG GIRL:	Sunday's daughter
PITRAS:	District agent of OLAF, another trading company, an expatriate

The Last Slave Traders

SIMEON:	An indigene employed by OSCA

LAURENT:	The name of the new man who has become Managing Director of OSCA

GRANIER JUNIOR:	An expatriate

INDIGENOUS EMPLOYEES,
CUSTOMERS, POLICEMAN
AND WORKERS.
EXPATRIATE EMPLOYEES.

Act 1, Scene 1

(The introducer stands on the stage in front of the curtain which is yet to rise)

THE INTRODUCER: The action is taking place in black Africa before and after the 1939 - 45 war. People from all walks of life were then swooping down on the African continent, like a swarm of locusts... Ruffians and boot lickers were getting on well and a new race of slave traders emerged.

(The curtain rises and the introducer takes leave) We are in the office of OSCA, a Trading Company in the area. There are finger-prints everywhere, and cobwebs on the ceiling. On the right is a lattice box through which one can see a European opposite the stage. A large door is open at the bottom, also facing the stage. One of those torrential, heavy rains, typical of the African coast during the rainy season, is falling. Far off on the right, a little door leads to the Manager's office which opens outside through another door.

In the office are about twenty blacks and five whites all of whom look stupefied. They are seated at tables placed near each other. Another white man is seated at a separate table near the little door. This office looks disorderly, dirty and uncomfortable. There are leaks in the roof and water falls at times when it rains hard. The workers look busy wiping their faces and arms. They are sweating profusely as there are no fans. Insects buzz noisily against the walls. From time to time a clapping of hands is heard. It's one of the workers trying to crush a mosquito or a fly.

From the office of Jadin, the Manager, loud noises emerge. The five Europeans and the native employees laugh on while making meaningful gestures, showing how happy they are to participate in the argument.

Granier, the sixth European, is alone at his table. He is middle-aged, bald, with detached ears, looking somehow stupid, a queer character with no personality.

He moves stealthily towards the door of the Manager's office. He sticks his ears to it and listens.

THE INTRODUCER: *(who has come back)* You are now right in the middle of the action, dear audience, now let me take leave of you. Bye bye! *(the introducer leaves and the curtain falls)*

ACT I

(the curtain rises)

SCENE I

GRANIER: *(making wide gestures)* What a licking he gives him! *(for some time gesticulating, and showing great joy)* What a licking! What a licking! Ha! ha! OK, now let's go back to our place, very slowly, very noiselessly! *(He returns slowly making the least possible noise. At the same time, the door opens, and a young black man, smallish in stature, appears, followed by the huge stature of Jadin, the Manager of OSCA, just like David and Goliath. Everybody, black or white, gets absorbed in work. There is total silence as though even the insects have stopped making noise)*

JADIN: *(moving towards Granier)* Granier! *(pointing to the young black man)* Take care of that bushman, he may prove helpful in our accounts department!

GRANIER: *(hurrying and looking obsequious and basely submissive)* Yes, Mr. Jadin.

JADIN: And get a move on!

GRANIER: As you direct, Mr. Jadin, *(curtsying twice)* as you wish, Mr. Jadin.

JADIN: Take care of him very well, do you understand? Not like the last one, OK? Put the screw on him this time!

GRANIER: *(making further curtsies)* As you wish, Mr. Jadin, at your service, Mr. Jadin.

JADIN: As I wish! As I wish! I hope so, Granier! Put the screw on all those idiots, both black and white. I'm fed up with all those bastards, yourself included! *(goes towards Granier and Granier jumps up and takes two steps backwards)* Do you hear me?

GRANIER: *(mumbling)* Yes, Mr. Jadin. At your service, Mr. Jadin. As you wish, Mr. Jadin.

JADIN: *(ironically)* Do you know what you are, Granier?

GRANIER: *(stammering more and more)* Yes, Mr. Jadin. No, Mr. Jadin I don't know, Mr. Jadin.

JADIN: You are a bloody idiot, Granier, a silly fucker!

GRANIER: Yes, Mr. Jadin. No, Mr. Jadin. Er, yes, Mr. Jadin. You are right Mr. Jadin. I am a bloody idiot, Mr. Jadin. A silly fucker, Mr. Jadin.

JADIN: *(going back, to his office)* Get lost you bloody fool! *(he slams the door behind him.)*

GRANIER: *(talking to himself)* I am a bloody idiot... That must be true, since Mr. Jadin says so... *(going back to his chair and shaking his head)* It must be true... *(seeing the young black man, and putting on a wicked look in his effort to imitate Jadin)* Are you still here? Follow me! A period of training at our accounts department will do you a lot of good. Yes, we are going to give you a good shake-up, you need it!

Act I, Scene II

THE YOUNG BLACK BOY: *(aloud)* I'll do my best sir! *(speaking off)* I'll remember the word bushman *(looking at the whites)*. They'll pay for it, all of them, especially Jadin that bush pig! One day *(glancing at Jadin's office)* I'll sit in his chair and then whites and blacks should better behave themselves!

(the curtain falls)

* * *

ACT I

(the curtain rises)

SCENE II

(enters by the main door a young long-haired man holding in one hand a guitar and in the other a little briefcase)

THE YOUNG POET: *(aside)* So that's it, this is OSCA. Well, it looks rather grim. How dark it is inside! Yet Africa is synonymous with light and sunshine! On which slave-ship do I find myself! I would nevertheless have made a good journey... Ah the sea! Blue meadow with thousands of flowers, a grandiose spectacle for ever renewing itself. I caught a bit of sea sickness, it is true, but Gisela made me quickly forget it. Oh the blue eyes of Gisela: two vivid jewels in a dear face! and her lips! Ah her lips... two red petals, where I drank honey. She is far now. Gone with the boat. The boat split the darkness of the night and the blue of the sea and separated us... But good God, what am I doing here? Is it a nightmare? *(crying)* Gisela! Gisela! am I awake? It is however day-time and the sun is high up in the sky. Gisela! Gisela! where are you? *(a boat's siren sounds)* I've lost you Gisela... and what's left for me? The cruel sun outside that burns my skin, my eyes, everything! And this black cave where I see insects milling in darkness... My God, don't abandon me before men... I'm afraid... Yet I am not very demanding. I just want to live that's all! What do I need? A bit of money, just a little bit, lots of friendship, and love, yes love.... and the blue eyes of Gisela!

(shouts) Gisela! *(Jadin appears on the steps of his door)*

JADIN: *(angry)* Why is he howling like that? *(to Granier)* Granier, who is this idiot neighing under my windows?

GRANIER: *(shaken out of his slumber)* At your service Mr. Jadin, as you wish, Mr. Jadin, I'm a bloody idiot, Mr. Jadin.

JADIN: *(laughing aloud)* That's true, you know. But no more discussions, Granier. I have other things to do. Call that... that fool daring to neigh on the steps of my door. *(goes back to his office)*

GRANIER: *(moving towards the new comer and assuming a furious look)* What do you want, sir?

THE POET: Who is talking to me? What is this voice that

Act I, Scene II

	seems to be coming from the belly of the earth? Could it be a spirit? Judging by the voice it could only be an evil one!
GRANIER:	*(pulling his sleeve)* Sir! Sir!
THE POET:	The spirit is snatching me. Devil, stop it! It's Gisela I want! *(he frees himself)*
GRANIER:	*(going towards the office of Jadin and knocking timidly)* Mr. Jadin... Mr. Jadin... It's me, Granier...
JADIN:	*(howling so loudly that it is heard through the door)* Ah the bloody fuckers! Damn it! Stinking shit! Come in!
GRANIER:	*(opening the door, jumping backwards and talking to Jadin who cannot be seen but only heard from the steps of the door)* It's me, Mr. Jadin.
JADIN:	*(angry)* What else do you want, Granier? You are getting on my nerves after all. Come on, get in!
GRANIER:	*(almost begging)* Mr. Jadin, it's the new comer...
JADIN:	The new comer! The new comer! This business of the new comer has not been resolved yet? Granier, this is really lamentable!
GRANIER:	*(at attention)* Yes, Mr. Jadin. You are right, Mr. Jadin...
JADIN:	*(in a weary tone)* And so?
GRANIER:	Well, Mr. Jadin, the new comer has been talking to himself as if in a dream. As I tried to

7

shake him up, he pushed me rather hard, Mr. Jadin.

JADIN: And you didn't hit back? Idiot! Get away!

GRANIER: He also called me a spirit, Mr. Jadin, a spirit, imagine! With my twenty years experience in the company, me a spirit?

JADIN: *(to Granier, in a harsh voice)* Get out of here, Granier! Let's go and see the other idiot who talks to himself! *(moves towards the poet, ruffles Granier as he passes, making him fall headlong) (to Granier)* That will teach you to keep off the way. Idiot! *(to the poet)* So what is it you want?

THE POET: Another spirit? I can hear another voice much louder and more terrible. This voice is from the ocean, no doubt about that. Could it be the spirit of tempests?

JADIN: *(holding him by the arm)* Now are you going to answer, yes or no? (he shakes him hard)

THE POET: The spirit is grabbing me once again, but it is grabbing so hard, this time, leave me alone, will you! *(struggles to free himself)*

JADIN: To hell with your spirits!

THE POET: He is strong, this one. He must have come from the great depths of the ocean. *(coming back to himself)* Sir, I'm happy to see you. I'm looking for OSCA. Where's the Manager?

JADIN: There he is.

Act I, Scene II

THE POET: Where? *(looking around without seeing anybody)* But where? I can't see anybody.

JADIN: Right in front of you.

THE POET: You? Is it you, sir? *(points a finger at Jadin)*

JADIN: *(annoyed)* Yes, me. Are you deaf or a dunce?

THE POET: *(retreating with fear) (aside)* But that's the devil incarnate. See the wickedness in the eyes, and the cruelty in his smiles!

JADIN: And you, who are you? Surname, first name, date of birth, qualifications.

THE POET: Me?

JADIN: Yes, you!

THE POET: It's because... I don't know if I may come in... *(aside)* What a ferocious look! But it is above all his eyes that frighten me.

JADIN: So are you going to reply, yes or no? *(aside)* It's terrible the kind of rabble that the people of Paris send to me... Mad men, day dreamers who talk to themselves!

THE POET: I really don't know if I should enter your office or not. It's too dark in there. Besides it's so dirty, for somebody like me who likes only beauty. Besides your eyes...

JADIN: Your name for Christ's sake! *(aside)* I only want to check whether he's one of the people expected from Paris. If he is one of them, he has had it! I'll put him on the very first boat

	going to Marseilles.
THE POET:	*(aside)* Since he appears to want it so badly, I am going to tell him my name. May be he will leave me alone after that. *(aloud)* Marly Pierre, born in 1915... Son of Marly Andre of...
JADIN:	*(interrupting him)* That's enough! Wait a minute. *(consulting a list he has pulled out of his pocket) (aside)* He's the one, no doubt, Marly Pierre. *(aloud)* Ok., no need entering. I'm putting you on the same boat. *(his face beams up)* What I have seen of you is enough for me to make up my mind about you.
THE POET:	Me too, sir, I have seen enough of you!
JADIN:	*(taken aback)* What, what are you saying, you over there?
THE POET:	I said I have seen enough of you, sir. In particular, I've seen enough of your eyes. But keep me at least for one month...
JADIN:	*(howling)* Away! Get out! Out of here!
THE POET:	*(imploring)* Keep me for a month sir, so that I can see the country, and my Muse will be grateful to you.
JADIN:	*(pushing him)* Out! To hell with your Muse.
THE POET:	*(trying not to move)* Just a month, only a month, sir! So that I could show my father, my poor father that I tried!
JADIN:	*(pushing him brutally)* Get out of here, you

Act I, Scene III

damned stinking shit!

THE POET: In order also that I may have something to say about Africa...

JADIN: Not a single hour more; not even a minute. The first boat!

THE POET: Only a week, sir... for the sake of my Muse...

JADIN: Not a minute. Come on, pack out of here!

THE POET: A few days, for the sake of my father...

JADIN: *(seizing him by the collar)* Out! Out of here!

THE POET: For the sake of my Muse...

JADIN: *(red with anger, he pushes out the poet and follows him)* Out, I say, Get out of here, and quicker than that!

THE POET: For the sake of my father! *(They exit. We hear the howling of Jadin and the voice of the poet getting fainter and fainter, repeating intermittently "for the sake of my Muse", "for the sake of my father" and a round of insults)*

(the curtain falls)

ACT 1

(The curtain rises. Same background)

SCENE III

GRANIER: *(talking to himself)* What a licking he gave him! *(expressive gestures showing the stupidity of*

Granier) Yes indeed! Congratulations Mr. Jadin, at your service Mr. Jadin *(he curtsies)* *(pensive)* Did I really hear him say "stupid"? I think it was something else... Next time I will be more attentive. But whatever he said must be true! Such a man cannot be mistaken. *(At that very moment shooting is heard outside as well as loud shouts. Then the door opens, or rather is violently kicked open. A tall stout person emerges. He is wearing a hunting dress, linen gaiters, big hobnailed shoes, a huge white colonial helmet with a white veil around his neck. He has several cartridge punches slung across his shoulders.)*

THE HUNTER: *(very loud)* A lion! a lion! I've got it. Victory! *(he goes forward holding his gun which is still smoking)* Where's the manager? I want to break the news to him. A lion! He will be happy. *(he moves towards Granier)* Where's the manager?

GRANIER: The manager? He's over there *(pointing at the door)*.

THE HUNTER: Fine, thank you. I'm going there to give him the news.

GRANIER: What news?

THE HUNTER: The lion, of course! What other news were you expecting? *(He goes to Jadin's door and enters without knocking), (We then hear a loud noise coming from Jadin's office. All the workers, both black and white raise their heads and laugh)*

JADIN: The first boat, I told you! The first boat!

Act I, Scene III

THE HUNTER: Gently my friend, gently, or I'll get annoyed and put some lead into your buttocks. Do you know who you are talking to? I am a hunter... do you realise?

JADIN: *(howling)* The first boat, and immediately! I couldn't care less about hunting!

THE HUNTER: And a real one! Not a hunter shooting clay pigeons! So gently, gently my friend. If St. Hubert were to hear you, can you imagine...?

JADIN: Out, I say. The first boat! *(tries once again to push him out)*

THE HUNTER: By Nimrod, you called for it. *(pushes Jadin back towards the office)* Be informed that I'm not going to leave here without a good hunting spree in the country. Why the hell do you think I came to Africa?

JADIN: I warn you, I'm going to call the police.

THE HUNTER: The police? Go ahead, if you so wish, but as for St. Hubert....

JADIN: St. Hubert?

THE HUNTER: Yes, St. Hubert. He will pay you back in kind.

JADIN: So you refuse to go!

THE HUNTER: Yes, I refuse! Assure me first that I shall have my hunting safari and I'll see later.

JADIN: *(managing to free himself)* Granier! Granier!

GRANIER: *(rushing in)* Yes Mr. Jadin! At your service,

Mr. Jadin, I'm a bloody fool, Mr. Jadin! *(to himself)* Yes that's the very word he used... Fool!

JADIN: Call the police, quick! *(goes back to his office followed by the hunter)*

GRANIER: Yes, Mr. Jadin. At your service, Mr. Jadin, *(As he gets ready to go he collides with a black policeman coming in)*

THE POLICEMAN: *(in dark blue uniform made up of a rather long pair of shorts, a sleeveless shirt, dark puttees, black shoes, blue chechia)* Can I see the Manager?

GRANIER: Just a minute! *(goes to Jadin's office and knocks)*

JADIN: *(appearing at the doorway)* You are still there Granier? *(weary gesture)*

GRANIER: *(triumphant)* It's the police, Mr. Jadin...

JADIN: I'm coming. Give way. *(pushes Granier and goes towards the policeman)* *(to the policeman)* So you have come to arrest this devil?

THE POLICEMAN: Me? Which devil? Tell me sir!

JADIN: *(low)* How stupid he is! *(aloud, pointing at the hunter who is outside the office)* There he is!

THE POLICEMAN: That one? I don't know him, sir. Is he the "devil"? I have come for the ass...

JADIN: The ass?

THE POLICEMAN: Yes, the ass.

Act I, Scene III

JADIN: What donkey are you talking about? Watch it, or you'll go by the first boat... *(in a low tone)* Oh no! not for him. *(aloud)* Better get out of here, or I'll report you to your superiors.

THE POLICEMAN: *(trembling with fear)* Yes, Manager... the donkey, a staff of your firm...

JADIN: Hurry up. Don't waste precious minutes! *(aside)* This devil of a monkey is getting on my nerves, with his story of the donkey! To hell with him and his donkey.

THE POLICEMAN: I want to know which one of your staff has killed the donkey?

JADIN: *(annoyed and in a low tone)* To hell with this nigger! Some kicks in the arse are being wasted! *(aloud)* Killed?

THE POLICEMAN: Yes, by gun shot...!

JADIN: And so?

THE POLICEMAN: And... *(looking in the direction of the hunter still holding his gun)* I can see a gun in the hands of this man.

JADIN: *(realising how he can exploit this situation) (triumphantly)* There is your man, the one who killed the donkey.

THE HUNTER: Killed a donkey? I killed a lion. Watch your words, sir. I will not stand this defamation of character! The honour of a hunter is not to be toyed with, sir, especially of a hunter who is a member of the hunter's club of TILLOT-

	ON-RONGEANT! I, killing a donkey? I, who saw the lion attack me and roar? How could I have killed a donkey?
JADIN:	*(in a bossy tone)* Take him away. That's him! A few weeks in prison will teach him sense. He will in the end be ready to board the first boat. *(to the hunter)* Hunting? my foot!
THE HUNTER:	*(to the policeman holding his arm)* Don't you touch me. Paul Dussant can become wild, you know. *(He pushes back the policeman. The latter takes out a whistle from his pocket and blows it several times. About a dozen black policemen rush in, helmeted and armed with clubs. They surround the hunter and drag him away).* *(to Jadin while they drag him away)* I am satisfied... I've got my lion, but watch it. If you are in my way, St. Hubert and I will know how to deal with you.
JADIN:	*(talking to himself and rubbing his hands)* Let me see the list, yes! Paul Dussant is really a native of Tillot. Yet another one liquidated! It's no picnic! *(He goes into his office. All heads rise. Then he comes out again and all heads bow down.)* *(To Granier)* Granier! make them work, all these good-for-nothing! Both blacks and whites! and don't allow a single one to raise his head. I, Jadin, want profit and sweat for the money they earn, those idiots! *(to himself)* That's really no joke. Two thrown out the same day! *(rubbing his hands).* Whose turn is it now? I'm expecting four more according to

the letter from Paris. I hope they too will take the first boat. I enjoy throwing people out. It's such a joy to me. *(rubs his hands)* We must enjoy when we can, *(goes on rubbing his hands). (notices that Granier is still near him) (to Granier)* Granier! What are you doing there? Do I need to repeat? Get this bunch of idiots working, both blacks and whites. I have already said so.

GRANIER: Yes, Mr. Jadin. *(curtsies)* At your service, Mr. Jadin *(more curtsies)* I am a bloody fool, Mr. Jadin *(curtsies)* A silly fucker, Mr. Jadin...

JADIN: Worse than a fool, Granier!

GRANIER: Worse than a fool, Mr. Jadin *(new curtsies) (goes back to his seat and Jadin to his office, the latter's face is beaming with a broad smile).*

GRANIER: *(alone)* Oh how he roughed that man! Congratulations, Mr. Jadin! *(curtsying by himself)* I am a fool, Mr. Jadin, worse than a fool, Mr. Jadin! *(more curtsies)*

(the curtain falls)

ACT I

SCENE IV

(Same background, same atmosphere. It is still raining. Granier looks more stupid than ever. His head is between his hands and he is absorbed in calculations.)

The Last Slave Traders

GRANIER: *(mumbling)* Three and four, seven and one, eight and two, ten and three, fourteen... Oh no, twelve... no thirteen *(aloud)* Oh my head! Mr. Jadin is right. I must be born stupid. Let's see if this bunch of black and white idiots are working as hard as they should. *(He moves from table to table, glancing furiously, which makes him look even more ridiculous, then he goes back to his seat.) (Enters a young white man. He is bearded, and carries with him all the tools of a painter, easel, colour box, etc.)*

THE PAINTER: *(coming closer to Granier)* May I see the manager please?

GRANIER: *(without raising his head pointing at Jadin's office)* Over there! *(The painter goes, knocks and enters. He comes out almost immediately and falls flat on the ground. A loud noise from the easel and the colour box, turned upside down. One can see in the doorway the large foot of Jadin that had pushed him out).*

JADIN: *(yelling)* First boat! First boat! To hell with your painting! *(the door closes again loudly.)*

THE PAINTER: *(getting up with pains and gathering his tools)* Damned fool! Bastard! I haven't painted even a sunset! *(going to the door)* Brute! And I was hoping to find a patron in such an animal!

GRANIER: *(counting on his fingers)* One, two, three, *(laughing)* already three. *(Another young man enters, crew-cut. Blond hair, tall, looking athletic. He has in his hands different rackets, tennis,*

Act I, Scene IV

               badminton, squash and on his right shoulder a volley ball in a net.)

THE SPORTSMAN: *(going near Granier)* The manager, please. *(Without raising his head or saying a word, Granier points to Jadin's office. The sportsman goes, knocks and enters. He comes out almost immediately, and one can see the huge foot of Jadin which pushed him out. He didn't fall like the painter, being saved by his huge size.)*

JADIN: *(shouting menacingly)* First boat! First boat! Sports? my foot! *(Jadin's door slams shut)*

THE SPORTSMAN: *(Going to the exit, brushing the things he carries)* I didn't even have time to compete with the blacks who are such good sportsmen. What an idiot! And I was hoping to find in him a manager! *(goes out.)*

THE PLAYBOY: *(coming near Granier with a smile)* The manager, please!

GRANIER: Yet another one? *(without raising his head or saying a word, he points at the office of Jadin) (The playboy goes to the Manager's office, knocks and enters. He comes out almost immediately and falls flat. One can see the huge foot of Jadin that has pushed him out. He falls like the painter, since his medium size can't protect him. There is no smile on his face as he brushes his hindquarters)*

JADIN: *(remaining in his office, crying like a savage)* First boat! First boat! What do I care about love! *(The door of Jadin's office closes with a bang.)*

THE PLAYBOY: *(going to the exit still brushing his back)* Foolish man! He wouldn't even give me time to try the black women, who are such wonderful lovers! Miserable chap! And I was hoping to find in him an advisor!

GRANIER: *(counting on his fingers)* One, two, three, four, five... Well done, Mr. Jadin. One more and the number will be complete. At your service, Mr. Jadin *(he bows down)* I'm an idiot, Mr. Jadin, *(more curtsies)* Yes, this will complete the number since we are expecting six. Let's see if that's it... *(Counting on his fingers, one, two, three, four, five, six)* Yes exactly so. Mr. Jadin you are really great! *(showing his admiration in a foolish way)* Five in a single day, and the sixth, who will share the same fate, without doubt! *(At the same time a smallish young man appears in the opening, rather timid. He wears a grey pair of trousers, a white shirt and a brown jacket. On his head is a sort of huge white colonial helmet. He's been completely soaked in torrential rain whose noisy fall can be heard from the roofs as well as the shutters. He removes his helmet and wipes his face with a large handkerchief. At the same time there is the noise of yelling from Jadin's office. The door suddenly opens and a black man is thrown out through the door by a big kick in the back. Jadin can be heard and seen yelling insults, among which the word monkey features prominently, then the door slams again. During this period all the workers in the office, both black and white,*

Act I, Scene IV

work harder, their heads bowed. THE NEW MAN is still standing holding his helmet. He gives the impression he doesn't know whether he should go in or out... He scratches his head whilst making an expressive mime).

THE NEW MAN: *(to himself)* Shall I go in or go away? What a funny reception! This office is simply awful. It is hot and there are no fans. *(He wipes his forehead.)* When I recall what they told me in Paris! Ultramodern offices, very comfortable, pleasant atmosphere... Atmosphere? They must have been joking! *(He now decided to go in. He first passes in front of Granier, but suddenly stops.)* No! not this one. I am not going to talk to him. He is too ugly! *(continuing to move between the tables)* And his face, my God! The sort that can cause nightmares. *(talking to a bespectacled European near whom he is standing)* Good day, sir, I would like to talk to the manager.

THE EUROPEAN WEARING SPECTACLES: He's over there! *(pointing at the little office whose door has just closed)*

THE NEW MAN: *(looking in the direction of the finger)* Over there?

THE EUROPEAN WEARING SPECTACLES: Yes.

THE NEW MAN: *(stunned, taken aback and motionless)* Over there?

THE EUROPEAN WORKER: Yes, over there! That's what I said. *(one head after the other rises up)*

THE NEW MAN: Is it a good time to go in?

THE EUROPEAN WEARING SPECTACLES: Now or later, it's all the same. The old man is always equal to himself.

THE NEW MAN: It's disturbing to see people thrown out of an office through a door! *(He moves in the direction of the fateful door. Arriving there he stands motionless for sometime, then knocks gently and timidly without immediate success. Shortly, however, the door opens violently and the poor boy is hit right in the face. The shock of the sudden brutal attack pushes him against the wall. The huge bulk of Jadin moves about in the office. As he throws a heap of paper over the cashier's cage, the cashier, — a European, gets up and collects the scattered paper).*

(JADIN NOTICES THE NEW MAN STANDING AGAINST THE WALL)

JADIN: What is that one doing here? My goodness, is he eavesdropping? *(addressing him directly)* Could you tell me what you are doing here? And first, who are you?

THE NEW MAN: My name is Buisson. I just arrived from France by yesterday's boat.

JADIN: *(to himself)* That's it. He's the sixth man. *(to the new man)* Come into my office. *(both enter, with Jadin more or less pushing the new man. Jadin slams the door violently. A piece of plaster falls*

Act I, Scene IV

down. The new man goes out almost immediately, falling on the floor. One can see the huge foot of Jadin that has pushed him out, and hear Jadin howl).

JADIN: *(neighing)* First boat! First boat! I care not for... what... for eavesdropping! *(the door shuts once again)* (THE NEW MAN REMAINS DAZED NEAR THE DOOR, RUBBING HIS BACK.)

THE NEW MAN: What did I do? Eavesdrop? God knows I did no damned eavesdropping. I came to work myself, not to paint or hunt wild life, or black women, or do God-knows-what, like those who travelled with me on that boat... It's unfair. *(He moves towards the exit.)*

GRANIER: *(counting on his fingers)* One, two, three, four, five, six... yes that's it. The six have all come. Six in, six out, and with what speed! Congratulations Mr. Jadin! You are making progress Mr. Jadin! Four last month, six this month, and today is only the sixteenth! This man is a real champion, a great man, and my ambition is to become great like him! But he says I am a... a moron... Yes that's what he says... and that must be true, a big man like him cannot make mistakes! *(Jadin collides with a black employee as he rushes out of his office. The latter falls on all fours).*

JADIN: *(to Granier)* Granier! Run fast and catch the new man! Bring him dead or alive! Oh no, rather alive, he is recommended by Paris...

Can you believe it? It's he who delivered the letter. Then they'll begin to get worried in high places! Six this month, it's a bit too much. Let's wait for the next month.

(to Granier) Come on Granier, are you still here? Run and catch him, I said!

GRANIER: *(at attention)* Yes, Mr. Jadin, I'm running. Yes, Mr. Jadin I'm flying. *(He rushes out.)*

JADIN: *(all alone)* Yes, I'll resume next month. Two or three more, to keep going. Hunters, playboys, sportsmen, you just name it... I would be extra kind to keep them, but painters, poets.... artists... never... no way! I won't entertain any of these species here. That breed is too clever, too strong for me! What I want is to dominate both body and spirit, and to be able to dominate, I have to create a void around me. I, Jadin the Great! And I hold dominion in my kingdom of blacks and whites... With the blacks there's no problem... a few kicks in the bottom, salary cuts here and there, and the trick works! Not a single one stirs! The only things that matter to these monkeys are strength and money! So with me they get satisfaction. My height 1.85m, my weight 120kg. They can come near! Most of them tremble in their pants. And really I enjoy it. *(stops talking for a brief while and walks up and down.)* *(The telephone rings)*

JADIN: *(taking the call)* Hello, yes, the CIK? No, it's **not here**! But since I am telling you it's not

Act I, Scene IV

here... you monkey! The number of the CIK? You can go fucking, *(putting back the phone)* Silly buggers, taking me for an informations office! *(Coming back to his subject)* Ah what blessed times when a kick in the buttocks is worth so much gold! But how long will this last? No idea. So let's make hay while the sun shines! With the whites, it is even easier. They are 5,000km away from home... So they keep quiet and resigned? Maybe they think of it, dream about it, but as they have to pay for their return journey in case of resignation, and their salary is not enough to pay for it, *(he laughs)* so they have to stay for three years! And me Jadin the Great, during these three years I reign over them as an absolute king. I have them right under my thumb. I manage it by kicking them in the buttocks, threatening to send them back by the first boat, a bit of this, a bit of that, and they accept everything. If I sacked them, they wouldn't find a job with ease. Yes, somebody sacked creates a bad impression, so they come back. They are a famishing lot, miserable wretches, these guys! This is my chance! By eliminating the intelligent ones, I am only left with mediocres... and I am happy with them! Somebody like Granier for instance, he's a real pearl! A rock solid investment! He came back eight times! Where else could he go, this poor Granier? *(silence)* This fool called Granier, this clumsy Granier! But in actual fact, where is he, this idiot? *(shouts)* Granier!

The Last Slave Traders

                 Granier!

GRANIER: *(from far away)* I'm coming, Mr. Jadin, at your service, Mr. Jadin....

JADIN: Be a little quicker and smarter!

GRANIER: *(coming nearer)* At your service, Mr. Jadin, at your service...

JADIN: An order is an order and meant to be obeyed!

GRANIER: *(appearing, holding THE NEW MAN by the arm)* Yes, Mr. Jadin. An order is an order. Oh Mr. Jadin! *(a stupid smile on his lips)* What a good way of saying it!

JADIN: Enough!

GRANIER: Yes, Mr. Jadin, at your service, Mr. Jadin, I'm an...

JADIN: Didn't I say it's enough?

GRANIER: Yes, Mr. Jadin.

JADIN: So you have the new man? Is he here? Really here?

GRANIER: Yes, Mr. Jadin. I have him right here with me Mr. Jadin...

JADIN: *(to Granier)* Granier that's enough! Shut up! *(to the new man)* Do you promise never to eavesdrop again?

THE NEW MAN: *(looking weary)* Yes sir, I promise.

JADIN: I don't know why I've had pity on you, when

Act I, Scene V

                in fact you deserved a hundred times the first boat! I must be in a good mood! But take it from me you must obey me... Without question.

THE NEW MAN: Yes sir! Thank you sir!

JADIN: *(to himself)* I find it annoying to have to relate gently with such a client when I feel a thousand times like kicking him in his little buttocks. Ah, these people in Paris! Can't they send their sons, grandsons, cousins and what-have-you, elsewhere rather than here? After all, Africa is so large!

                Now my boy! See Mr. Granier! He will initiate you into the work.

GRANIER: Yes, Mr. Jadin. Surely, Mr. Jadin. At your service, Mr. Jadin. I am a... Mr. Jadin...

                (The curtain falls)

ACT I

SCENE V

Gaming Room at Jadin's house. An aunt sally game stands near a ping pong table and a game of darts. Jadin standing throw balls made of cloth at swinging wooden dolls. Two of them represent white, four other black men. Each has a name printed on them.

JADIN: *(sipping a whiskey)* This room is where I really feel at home and practise my favourite pastime aunt sally game. It's incredible how it works off my frustrations and each ball I throw is just like a slap in the face or a kick in the arse given to one of the blokes at my service, whether white or black! *(throwing a ball with all his strength at one of the white doll)* For you Granier, right in your mug! *(shouting with joy)* I got him! I got him! His head has tipped over! Ah Granier you got it right in your dirty mug! It's unbelievable how I detest, how I hate that chap! I hate him all the more so since he is the boot licking type! However I wonder if it is not disgust he inspires in me rather than hatred. *(looking at the other white head)* As to that one, Laurent's own, it's really hatred it inspires in me, hatred slightly tinged with fear and admiration! *(throwing a ball at the doll figuring Laurent)* He is exactly the opposite of Granier... Oh I missed it! My God this bastard diverts the balls! As much one, spineless to the extreme, crawls to any form of authority, as much the other is rebellious to any form of injustice wherever it may come from! *(throwing a second ball and shouting)* Shit, I missed again! This time I touched his head but it did not move! That's quite him, the bastard! Rigid. Stiff as a poker, that's how he is and not inclined to bow and scrape to anybody! Well now let's hit the black mugs! *(throwing with all his strength a ball at one of the four black heads! and at first the one of Ekpeniong the transit clerk whom I despise particularly! (shouting with joy)*

Act I, Scene V

	I got the bastard and at the first throw! *(pointing to the doll representing Ekpeniong)* Eh Ekpeniong, you got it right in your dirty mug didn't you? I dislike all these blokes white or black, crawling at my feet or trampling on authority! My hatred is all on edge just seeing them! I am a misanthropist for sure, coupled with a wicked and perverse person who derives pleasure doing evil. A sadist, that's the right word and that's what I am!
GRANIER:	*(who has come in unnoticed)* A sadist, that's what you are Mr. Jadin! And it must be true since that's what you say! A great man like you cannot make a mistake! As to me I am a bloody fool, Mr. Jadin! At your service, Mr. Jadin... a bloody fool, Mr. Jadin! But I would like so much, Mr. Jadin to be a sadist as well, just like you! I don't know the meaning of that word but it must be something good since you are one, Mr. Jadin!
JADIN:	*(who at last realises that Granier is around)* What the bloody hell are you doing here?
GRANIER:	Nothing Mr. Jadin. I am a bloody fool, Mr. Jadin! Nothing except to see how you spend your spare time! I am a bloody fool Mr. Jadin.
JADIN:	*(shouting)* What! What do you say?
GRANIER:	My dream is to become like you Mr. Jadin, I admire you so much Mr. Jadin and that's why at the office I do my best to imitate you and act just as you do! Then now, I long to do

	at home what you do at your place, this way, imitating you in everything Mr. Jadin.
JADIN:	*(howling and besides himself with anger)* Get the hell out of here! Bloody hell I am at home here, it's no public place! The hell with your admiration and imitation! *(grabbing his arm and trying to push him outside)* Out I say and fuck off!
GRANIER:	*(struggling like one possessed) (faintly)* Yes I admire you Mr. Jadin. You are a sadist Mr. Jadin and my only desire is to become one, to be just like you Mr. Jadin!
JADIN:	*(shouting more than ever and shaking Granier)* A sadist, me? Granier how do you dare!
GRANIER:	Yes, you Mr. Jadin. I am a bloody fool, Mr. Jadin! At your service, Mr. Jadin! A real bloody fool, Mr. Jadin, waiting to be a sadist, just as you are, Mr. Jadin!
JADIN:	*(pushing him brutally outside and kicking him in the arse)* Fuck off Granier, swing and fall just like the doll of my aunt sally game!
GRANIER:	*(who loses his balance and falls)* I am a bloody fool, Mr. Jadin! At your service, Mr. Jadin.

(The curtain falls)

ACT I

(The curtain rises)

SCENE VI

A fortnight later. Same background, same characters. The new man is sitting near Granier. He appears to be very busy. So also do the other workers, both black and white. The door of Jadin's office is open. Jadin appears holding a huge heap of papers. He goes first towards Granier's office and throws to him part of the heap.

JADIN: There, Granier! There's work for you and your zebras! It must be impeccable, eh! Profit, Granier! Press for profits! You don't work satisfactorily in this office. Time doesn't mean much to you, even though the proverb "Time is money" is well known, indeed.

GRANIER: Yes, Mr. Jadin. *(stammering)* Impeccable, profit, time, yes Mr. Jadin!

JADIN: Enough of that, Granier!

GRANIER: *(at attention)* Yes, Mr. Jadin, yes, Mr. Jadin.

JADIN: I'm really fed up. Get that into your head. Time cannot be regained, once lost. To think that I pay all these good-for-nothing fellows for doing nothing!

GRANIER: Oh yes, Mr. Jadin. You're right Mr. Jadin.

JADIN: And I include you, Granier, among the good-for-nothing *(he moves towards Granier, with a threatening look)*

GRANIER:	*(withdrawing instinctively)* You are right, Mr. Jadin. At your service, Mr. Jadin. *(weeping tone)* I am an imbecile, Mr. Jadin, a silly bugger. *(All the other workers are seriously absorbed in their work. The new man doesn't know where to fit himself. He tries to hide behind a huge accounting book which he has opened in-- front of him.)*
JADIN:	I've decided to do one thing.
GRANIER:	*(still at attention)* Yes, Mr. Jadin.
JADIN:	Shut up. I'm not talking to you. *(Granier regains his seat. Jadin walks up and down and when he comes near a worker whether black or white, the latter jumps up, visibly frightened.)* I've decided to buy a big clock, an enormous clock, all black with big white figures. I would have preferred the figures to be black too as I want these blockheads to see everything in black colour, but it's not possible. I'll have it hung in a conspicuous place so that these hopeless guys realise that time is money. I'm going to teach them time sense, as rapidly as possible. *(to Granier)* Granier! *(Granier doesn't hear, and continues working)* Granier! Am I not talking to you?
GRANIER:	Yes, Mr. Jadin. At your service, Mr. Jadin.
JADIN:	It is not enough being an imbecile, you've become deaf, too? Call me when they bring the clock.

Act I, Scene VI

GRANIER: Yes, Mr. Jadin. As you like, Mr. Jadin. *(Jadin goes to his office and enters. Soon a certain degree of relaxation shows among the workers. The new man drops the huge book with which he hides his face, and shows up again. He takes out a handkerchief and wipes his forehead. Jadin's door opens suddenly and he takes a few steps in the main office, a pile of papers in his hands. From far he throws the pile of papers on to the cashier over the cage and all the papers scatter on the ground. The cashier, on all fours, picks up the papers, one after the other. All the workers once again get seriously absorbed in their work. As soon as Jadin's door closes the same relaxed atmosphere dawns among the workers.)*

THE NEW MAN: *(wiping his forehead and talking to himself)* I would never have imagined Africa from this angle. *(wipes his forehead once again)* It's fifteen days since I came. It's not much but in fifteen days, I've seen so much ignominy, so much mental depravity and so much meanness, all in the same man! *(looks in the direction of Jadin's office)* Such moronic condition, such stupidity, such degradation! *(looking at Granier)*. Such apathy! *(pointing with a circular gesture to the other employees)* I must react against these, or *(looking at Granier)* I would become like him. *(The door of Jadin's office opens... and he comes out like an arrow, as usual. He passes in front of the new man without even noticing him, and moves towards a black employee. The new man tightening his fists takes a few steps behind him, then, his head bowed, he goes back to his seat.)*

THE NEW MAN: *(to himself)* I'm not ready yet... but tomorrow....

JADIN: *(passing in front of Granier)* What about the clock, Granier? Any news?

GRANIER: *(with a start)* No, Mr. Jadin! No, Mr. Jadin! At your service, Mr. Jadin. *(Jadin goes back to his office)*

THE NEW MAN: *(lowering his head)* Yes, tomorrow. . . perhaps. . .

(The curtain falls)

ACT II

(The curtain rises)

SCENE I

(Same decors — Same characters) (some indigenous workers enter the office carrying a huge black clock with white hands. They come near Granier)

FIRST BLACK WORKER: *(talking to Granier)* We've brought the clock, sir.

GRANIER: *(jumping with surprise)* Yes, Mr. Jadin, you are right, Mr. Jadin. I am a ... *(raising his head and seeing the two black workers)* Oh, what do you want?

SECOND BLACK WORKER: We've brought the clock, sir... It is really beautiful, sir...

GRANIER: We don't need the comments of a nigger like you. Watch it, eh! Or you leave by the first boat!

FIRST BLACK WORKER: You are right, Oga sah! A black man's observations are not important.

GRANIER: *(to the blacks)* Look, leave me alone. Wait over there. Go back! *(He pushes them, kicking them in the buttocks.)* Go back you niggers! *(to himself)* If Mr. Jadin could see me, he would be so happy! I am behaving exactly like him. Two kicks in the buttocks... I am going to give each of them another one *(pushing a step*

The Last Slave Traders

towards the blacks). Come on, move you dirty niggers, *(clumsily, he kicks each of them. The two blacks retreat and wait humbly, their heads bowed down. Granier finally goes towards Jadin's office and stops outside. He pricks up his ears, putting them close to the door, brushes his clothes and hair in a funny mimicry. The door opens suddenly and Granier finds himself pushed against the wall. Jadin emerges.)*

JADIN: So you too are eavesdropping eh! It's a real disease! What about the clock, Granier! the clock! Oh! Oh! *(angrily)* Why are you so tongue-tied? Will you answer? Was it not enough for you to be a deaf blockhead? Now you must be dumb as well!

GRANIER: *(stammering)* Yes, Mr. Jadin... No, Mr. Jadin, oh! I'm confused, Mr. Jadin! You're right, Mr. Jadin, oh yes, the clock, Mr. Jadin!

JADIN: Yes, the clock, you bloody fool.

GRANIER: *(shaking and stammering).* It is... it is... it is there... *(he points at it)* Mr. Jadin.

JADIN: There it is! My beautiful clock, all black, except for the hands. Pity they couldn't be black too. I want to give the blues to all those imbeciles. They'll see. I'm going to give them something to worry about. What do they think? That they came to the African coast to enjoy themselves? I'm going to put into their heads not only terrible ideas but also terrible dreams, and nightmares. Those idiots

Act II, Scene I

thought they were going to be happy here! Fools! who came only for the sunshine and the blue sky. I am going to give them a funny kind of sunshine! A black sun, that's what I have for them. *(He walks up and down)* That's good for the whites. As for the blacks... Well they are already black inside and outside. What else could be in their heads other than black? The black of perfect imbecility and of stupidity. Ah Jadin! You were born too late. You would have been the captain of a slave ship, a whip in your hand, lashing at naked black skins. I only have an office in place of a boat, with about thirty men in guise of crew... and slaves. That was unheard of. There is of course the white slavery... but it happens only to women. I have no whip, no! But I have my feet and my words. Often a word does more harm than a kick. *(stopping suddenly in front of the two blacks)* The two of you, go over there and hang the clock! *(shows them a place on the wall)*

THE TWO BLACK WORKERS: *(in a single voice)* Yes sir! *(terrified by Jadin, and almost trembling)* Yes sir, Ogah!

JADIN: *(in an angry tone)* There! I told you higher up... No, lower down.

THE TWO BLACK WORKERS: Yes sir!

JADIN: Not so high! Oh what dimwits! There, I am

telling you. For Christ's sake! Lower down! *(There follows a very funny scene in which the clock is fixed either too high or too low by the two terrorised black workers), (to himself)* Bloody niggers *(to the black workers)* There, I am telling you! A pack of block heads, that's what you are! I'm fed up! *(tearing his hairs)* fed up with monkeys like you!.

THE TWO BLACK WORKERS: *(more and more scared)* Yes sir! *(almost weeping)* Yes sir!

JADIN: *(raising his arms to the sky)* Damn it! There, I say. *(The two blacks, seeing the raised arms of Jadin, misinterpret his intentions, suspect that he is going to hit them. They drop the clock, which falls down with a huge metallic noise.)*

THE TWO WORKERS: *(running as fast as their legs can carry them)* He go kill us o!

JADIN: *(his arms pointing to the sky)* Damn it! my clock! my wall clock! and these two clowns running away! and the kicks in their arses which I can't deliver!!! *(getting more and more carried away, he gets into delirium tremens talking to nobody in particular.)* I'm alone here. Do you all hear me? I'm alone as if in a desert. *(all, except Granier, are absorbed in their work with a lot of zeal.)* You will slowly kill me! You fools! All of you, whites, blacks, new, old, everybody, even Granier, that dunderhead of an eavesdropper! *(to himself)* They want to kill me, I can feel it! they are ruffians *(all)* without

Act II, Scene II

exception! (aloud) Yes, all of you! *(sweeps the room with a gesture)* Ruffians pretending to work, while in reality you have sworn to ruin me! I clearly see through your little game! Don't think that I am taken in! He who laughs last laughs best! We shall see who has the last word. *(the clock begins to strike)* Even the clock betrays me! Oh what an abomination! What have I done to the gods to deserve such a fate on earth? Alright! I'll go away. I'll leave the place for you, you swines! whipper-snippers! niggers! pale faces! *(moves towards his office and seizes a pile of papers as he passes Granier's desk) (aloud)* Listen! all of you without exception, you are worth nothing to me, nothing more than these sheets of paper *(he tears them to pieces and throws them into the air)*. Not more than these pieces of paper flying away... *(goes back to his office, slamming the door violently. (The clock strikes once again).*

(The curtain falls)

ACT II

(The curtain rises)

SCENE II

(Same background. Same characters. The clock is fixed on the wall).

THE NEW MAN: *(standing near his table) (speaking off)* Well, this Jadin man exaggerates and goes too far! He's crazy, no more, no less. The sun and whisky have had the better part of him. The poor guy sees enemies everywhere, when in fact everybody is scared stiff of him, myself included... Hum! hum! *(coughs)* That's how I postpone my plan of action from day to day. and I don't do anything except talking nonsense! This bully frightens me, that's all. He is a slave trader, the bastard! Just like all the managers of these trading companies. Where are the high salaries? The modern flats? The pleasant atmosphere. The managements full of understanding? All that is no more than wind! We have been caught in a trap! Sailing in a slave ship, going God-knows-where! All that because of a rather attractive advertisement, in a supposedly responsible daily. *(takes a step forward)* Good God! you have to get out of it as quickly as possible. But how? May be tomorrow? Yes, tomorrow! *(going back to his table)* You are just as cowardly as the others!

JADIN: *(talking to Granier)* Granier, I hope that you have spoken to the new chap about the overtime in the evening and Sunday morning. I have seen him three times already leaving this office at exactly five o'clock, when I, Jadin, close at seven! Besides that, this little gentleman did not come last Sunday morning like everybody!

GRANIER: Yes, Mr. Jadin, I've already told him. But I'm going to remind him. He may have forgotten, Mr. Jadin.

Act II, Scene II

JADIN: *(low)* Forgotten? Idiot! My staff forgetting what I say! *(he goes to the far end of the office... Granier whispers to the new man with gestures. Jadin comes back and enters his office. It is 5.00 p.m. The clock strikes five times. Nobody moves except the new man who goes toward the exit. Jadin leaves his office for the second time, looks at the clock and counts the number of employees. He spots the empty seat of the new man.) (furious)* I told you, Granier, to give the new man a second warning!

GRANIER: Yes, I did Mr. Jadin! *(stammering)* Mr. Ja... Jadin, I have told... told him a second time...

JADIN: Go and bring him at once. He will understand, the fucker. *(Granier goes out hurriedly).*

JADIN: *(talking to himself)* Incredible! This is the first time it's happened to me. Challenge my orders... Well, we'll see.

GRANIER: *(out of breath)* He's coming, Mr. Jadin. He will first drink his cup of tea and take a little walk.

JADIN: Is that what he said?

GRANIER: Yes, Mr. Jadin... Sure Mr. Jadin! He said something else *(behaves like a shy little boy).*

JADIN: What was it, Granier?

GRANIER: *(simpering)* I can't, Mr. Jadin... It is so indecent, Mr. Jadin!

JADIN: Really? Tell me by Jove or I will extract it

The Last Slave Traders

                from you by force.

GRANIER: I can't, Mr. Jadin. It is so indecent, Mr. Jadin!

JADIN: Whisper it to me then, but first of all am I father and a mother to you all, or just anybody?

GRANIER: A father, Mr. Jadin, *(gets on to his toes, places his hand in the form of a horn on the ear of Jadin. He's heard uttering to Jadin the famous indecent word)* "Bloody Jadin is a pain in the neck, a real drag!" That's what he said, Mr. Jadin. You can now understand why I couldn't pronounce such indecent words before everybody.

JADIN: *(taken aback)* Good heavens. This is incredible! This is the very height of impoliteness! Bloody hell! *(the new man enters the office, with his hands in his pockets, whistling, and moving towards Jadin's office).*

THE NEW MAN: *(speaking to Jadin)* Did you send for me, Mr. Jadin?

JADIN: *(aloud)* I think so! *(in a low tone)* This little fellow is pulling my legs!

THE NEW MAN: What can I do for you, sir?

JADIN: *(stupefied)* So you pretend not to know why I sent for you?

THE NEW MAN: *(looking innocent)* I have no idea, sir.

Act II, Scene II

JADIN: *(talking to himself)* May be this dolt of Granier did not explain things to him properly. Let us see! *(to the new man)* What about overtime, young man? What do you do with it? Look at your colleagues!

THE NEW MAN: Overtime? I hate it, Mr. Jadin. I don't even want to hear about it. As for these people... *(pointing to the other employees)* I don't want to know them!

JADIN: *(talking to himself)* Incredible! Never did anybody ever talk to me like this. But may be he's drunk! *(to the new man)* Do you realise the implications of what you are saying?

THE NEW MAN: Surely, sir.

JADIN: Are you by any chance drunk?

THE NEW MAN: Me drunk? I never take alcohol!

JADIN: Say that you are drunk, and I shall be quits with you!

THE NEW MAN: Not a single drop of alcohol enters my mouth, sir!

JADIN: I entreat you, young man. Tell me you have drunk something....

THE NEW MAN: Not a drop, sir!

JADIN: Come on! A good sign. Just a glass...

THE NEW MAN: I've told you I haven't drunk anything!

JADIN:	Only a little drop, everybody does that! Come on!
THE NEW MAN:	Nothing!
JADIN:	Not a drop, you maintain?
THE NEW MAN:	Not a single drop.
JADIN:	*(alone)* Then I'm finished.... It's the end of the world... The earth is revolving... quickly... quickly... and I am falling... I'm falling... into an abyss *(he falls headlong)*.

(and the curtain falls, very slowly).

ACT II

(the curtain rises)

SCENE III

Jadin's office, a room much smaller than the other one, clean and well-lit. A ceiling fan and a table fan, both working. A black man near Jadin fanning him. A black worker is busy digging a hole in the wall adjacent to the big office. From time to time he casts a timid look at Jadin. Jadin is seated opposite the stage. He's smoking an enormous cigar and rocking himself in his armchair, his fingers in his waist-coat.

JADIN:	*(to himself)* The bad dream has disappeared, but I really thought it was all over, that Jadin was no more. But after a good sleep, the phoenix has resurrected itself. With this little hole in the wall, the profits are going to

Act II, Scene III

double. They wouldn't know when I'm spying *(takes a puff at his cigar)*. As for this little idiot of a new comer, ah, ah, ah! This little imbecile who is bold enough to refuse to do overtime! Ah! ah! He is simply going to disappear. I'm going to dispatch him to a distant, hot corner of the country, right in the bush, where he will learn to know the blessings of the sun, since Paris seems interested in the boy and I cannot give him the sack! It would be madness to keep him here. He will contaminate all the other block-heads. *(howling to the black worker)* Will it soon be over?

THE BLACK WORKER: *(terrorised)* Yes, sir, it's over.

JADIN: *(to the black worker)* It's about time too, you monkey, breaking my ear-drums for so long You are lucky I am in a good mood today *(he moves towards the hole and bends to take a look)*. *(to himself)* OK. I can see them. They are all busy of course, since they know I can see them through the hole. It's an excellent device, is it not? *(rubs his hands, takes big puffs at his cigar, then observes that the scared black worker is still there)*. *(to the black worker)* What? You are still around?

THE BLACK WORKER: Yes sir, yes sir, I am going, Oga sah!

JADIN: *(to the black workder)* Fast! My feet on your buttocks will do you a lot of good! *(opens the door, pushes the black man out, rewarding him with a kick in the lower region of his back.) (there's*

The Last Slave Traders

a big crowd outside) (alone) What are all these people outside? What do they all want from me today? Let me first watch them through the hole. *(he goes to the hole)* Perfect. The crowd is made of only customers and all my "Zebras" are working quietly just like sheep! *(laughs)* Ah! ah! ah! Sheep... sheep... And I am the wolf. *(striking his chest).* I...

(someone knocks at the door)

JADIN: *(yelling)* Come in! *(a young black girl aged between fifteen and sixteen enters... hesitating) (in a softened tone)* Good morning my child!

THE YOUNG BLACK GIRL: Good morning, sir.

JADIN: *(aloud)* I like children you know. *(in a low tone)* In a rather special way. Am I not after all the wolf?

THE YOUNG BLACK GIRL: I've been sent by my father. He just said that you may be pleased to see me...

JADIN: *(moving nearer and examining her in detail from head to toe)* Who is your father? *(continuing to examine her).*

THE YOUNG BLACK GIRL: My father is SUNDAY, one of your employees in the Transit Department.

JADIN: Sunday? That old fool is your father?

THE YOUNG BLACK GIRL: Yes sir.

JADIN: *(continuing his inspection, goes very close, eyes her covetously and ventures a peep into the open-*

Act II, Scene III

    ing of the girl's dress) Well, I'm happy to see you. Really very happy. You can tell Sunday. *(aside)* Very happy, indeed, but I shall be happier still when... oh, oh! anyway, we shall see! and soon... *(aloud)* You will tell your father to come and see me. Eh!

THE YOUNG BLACK GIRL: Yes sir.

JADIN: Bye bye, my child. *(taps her on the buttocks)*

    (she goes out) (alone) For heaven's sake. If I had any sense eh! for heaven's sake, I would neglect work for a whole hour! She's very young, she's well-shaped... *(makes suggestive gestures).* Ah good heavens! For Christ sake! for heaven's sake! *(takes long strides in the office)* Anyway we'll see about that later. I'll talk to this old idiot Sunday this very evening. *(continues walking up and down without talking for a few minutes).* Let me go and see my "Zebras" *(goes to the wall).* They are still working, good. My trick is wonderful, fantastic! *(lights another cigar and puffs copiously)* Yes! fantastic, my trick. *(somebody knocks at the door leading outside). (howling)* Come in *(a black old man enters. He is completely bent with age and could be eighty years old).*

THE OLD BLACK MAN: Good morning Mr. Boss!

JADIN: *(threatening)* Who are you? *(to himself)* Whoever you are, you don't have long to live.

THE OLD BLACK MAN: It's me, Alexander, the old cook of OSCA.

The Last Slave Traders

JADIN: Ah it is you Alexander? Are you not dead yet?

ALEXANDER: Eh! no!

JADIN: What do you want? You've been getting on my nerves for so many years! Aren't you ashamed to be still alive, an old idiot like you?

ALEXANDER: *(who has not understood the insult)* I came to say good morning, Mr. Boss, for tomorrow is the 14th of July, the French national day, and as we are both on a foreign soil...

JADIN: I don't need any greetings from an old monkey like you. As for your 14th of July, I care least for it if you want to know. First, the 14th of July is only meant for whites and not for old baboons like you. See that old baboon who thinks the 14th of July is for one of his kind! If you think you are French you are deceiving yourself, my poor chap! The Republic couldn't care less for an old bastard like you in her ranks! You understand?

ALEXANDER: But in the past I fought in Madagascar... for France...

JADIN: What do I care about your fight? Get out of here.

ALEXANDER: *(tears in the eyes)* Well, sir, *(moves, bent double, to the door)*.

JADIN: As a matter of fact, don't you have some daughters or grand-daughters?

Act II, Scene III

ALEXANDER: *(weeping)* No sir, I am alone in this world.

JADIN: No grand-daughters or grand-nieces?

ALEXANDER: No sir.

JADIN: Get out then, and die quickly so that I don't see you again. But coming to think of it, the company pays you pension...

ALEXANDER: Yes sir, 1,000 Frs. a month

JADINE: *(alone)* I'm going to do everything necessary.

ALEXANDER: Sir?

JADIN: Nothing. Get out of here!

ALEXANDER: Bye bye, Mr. Boss. *(he leaves)*

JADIN: *(alone)* I'm going to do everything necessary, yes. I'm going to stop the payment of his retirement benefits, no more, no less. That way, he will die quickly. That will reduce general expenses. *(puffs violently at his cigar.)* But let us see my chaps *(goes towards the hole in the wall)* Incredible! all at work! *(again he puffs at his cigar) (Someone knocks at the door leading outside) (yelling)* Come in *(to himself)* But why do they all want to see me this morning? *(a middle aged black man comes in).* Oh it's you, Sunday.

SUNDAY: You sent for me, sir?

JADIN: Me? No! And you know it very well, old scamp?

SUNDAY: I swear, sir, I thought you were calling me.

The Last Slave Traders

JADIN:	It doesn't matter. I've seen your daughter... So, agreed! You will bring her to me this evening, OK?
SUNDAY:	Yes sir, I'll bring her to your house at around 9.00 pm., if you permit, sir...
JADIN:	Not 9.00! 10.00 o'clock is better. I eat and drink, you know! Everything at its time! By the way, Sunday, how old is your daughter?
SUNDAY:	She'll be fifteen this year.
JADIN:	Fifteen? Oh!
SUNDAY:	And you will be the first, sir!
JADIN:	The first? I see! *(to himself)* Great! *(to Sunday)* You are sure?
SUNDAY:	Sure, sir, very sure! As sure as... as my body is standing before you!
JADIN:	OK Sunday, I'm pleased with you. Have no fears, you'll receive a handsome gift.
SUNDAY:	Thank you sir...
JADIN:	Sunday, how many more daughters do you have?
SUNDAY:	Three, sir...
JADIN:	Three! And are they all as young as this one?
SUNDAY:	Yes sir, one is fourteen years old, another is thirteen, and the youngest is twelve.
JADIN:	Very good, very good, Sunday! I can see you

Act II, Scene III

	getting a promotion! *(alone)* This rejuvenates me! And of course, it's not bad to be the first one!
SUNDAY:	Thank you sir, thank you!
JADIN:	Yes, I'll see you tonight, Sunday, with the eldest. *(Sunday goes out).*
JADIN:	*(alone)* At least this one knows how to make use of his daughters. Ah the large families! If the others are as pretty as this one, they could take turns... this one today, that one tomorrow, and I would take a rest on Sundays. Sunday is the resting day for the wolf! *(bursts out laughing)* I am the wolf! *(somebody knocks again at the door but this time at the door leading to the main office) (howling)* Come in *(low tone)* But it's a procession! *(Granier comes in)*
GRANIER:	Good morning, Mr. Jadin. My best wishes, Mr. Jadin, my greetings... My...
JADIN:	*(snarling)* Enough, please! Enough! What else do you wish me!
GRANIER:	Mr. Jadin... it's a serious issue!
JADIN:	Serious?
GRANIER:	Yes, Mr. Jadin...
JADIN:	*(interrupting him)* What is it again? Explain yourself quickly, I have no time to lose.
GRANIER:	Mr. Jadin... The bachelors made a lot of noise last night. They march, they walk, Mr. Jadin,

	they march in their room. I don't know what's wrong with them... And this gets on the nerves of my wife... Mr. Jadin... You know Mrs. Granier, Mr. Jadin... So...
JADIN:	So?
GRANDIER:	So I thought you could stop it, Mr. Jadin, that noise of footsteps, ... that regular noise of footsteps in the room!
JADIN:	It's easy, very easy! I'm going to order them not to walk again, not on their feet at least. They may crawl or walk on their heads.
GRANIER:	*(clapping hands)* You are right, Mr. Jadin, let them walk on their heads!
JADIN:	Go and bring them all, Granier, into my office, and very quickly!
GRANIER:	Yes, Mr. Jadin! Immediately, Mr. Jadin! On their heads, Mr. Jadin! *(goes out)*
JADIN:	*(alone)* It's not that I'm interested in Granier or his wife. In fact I couldn't care less about them and their sleep, but that will give me another chance to tame this bunch of idiots. *(somebody knocks at the door.)* Come in. *(Granier enters, followed by all the European employees including the new comer)* *(to Granier)* Are they all here?
GRANIER:	Yes, Mr. Jadin. All here, Mr. Jadin.
JADIN:	*(talking to all the young European employees)* Mr. Granier, your elder and senior, is com-

Act II, Scene III

>plaining about the noise you make in your rooms. You know that your rooms are located just above the six rooms of Mr. Granier. So I don't want any more noise, do you hear? Mr. Granier hears footsteps, I want them stopped. Don't walk again, not on your feet anyway. Walk on your heads, walk as you please, but no more noise! I hope you've understood me well.

THE NEW MAN: How can you prevent us from walking in your hole of a place. We are all in cells, not in rooms! Your cells measure 4 x 4 metres without running water and fans, how can we help walking?

JADIN: Please keep quiet, young idiot!

THE NEW MAN: *(continuing)* 4 metres by 4, and all white washed, and only one 15 watts bulb on the ceiling, yes 15 watts because these are not 10 watts bulbs and I repeat, no fan! We are not like you who have two fans in his office and a slave to fan him!

JADIN: Aren't you going to shut up?

THE NEW MAN: I'll not keep quiet till I've finished what I have to say! I have too much on my heart! Look *(opens the outside door and one can see rain falling very heavily)* at the rain outside. Where do you want us to walk, if not in your 4 x 4 rooms? One couple has six rooms, whereas the rest of us are no different from caged lions.

JADIN:	*(to himself)* He wants to beat me, the little runt! He compares himself to a lion when I see myself as a wolf. *(aloud)* You had better shut up. You are the only one complaining. Your colleagues don't say anything.
THE NEW MAN:	They are too stupefied by your threats to react.
JADIN:	*(addressing the group)* Isn't it true gentlemen that you are very happy with your lot?
THE GROUP:	*(all in once voice)* Yes, Mr. Jadin!
JADIN:	*(to the new man)* As you can see, all these people are happy!
THE NEW MAN:	You have made them too stupid to react anymore. Your methods have yielded fruits. Congratulations! You are an authority in taming and brain washing.
JADIN:	*(to the new man)* You will hear from me, very soon, young man! *(to all of them)* That's OK. You can. *(they all go except Granier) (to Granier)* So you are happy?
GRANIER:	Oh yes! Mr. Jadin, very happy. But Mrs. Granier will be so much happier to think that you have silenced this horde of little kids. She will be delighted! As if these young bachelors had the right to walk or even exist!
JADIN:	So you are happy?
GRANIER:	Ah yes! Mr. Jadin, very happy.

Act II, Scene III

JADIN: Alright. You can congratulate yourself for being utterly foolish! You did not even brief me about the character of the new man! That's how disasters start, Granier! *(shouting)* We let a little speck of sand enter into the machine, then one fine day, everything stops, and the Graniers find themselves out of work! Do you understand? *(moves towards Granier who retreats)* Is it understood?

GRANIER: *(shaking)* Yes, Mr. Jadin!

JADIN: *(to himself)* I'm sure this stupid ass did not understand anything. But it doesn't matter. We are going to eliminate the grain of sand. *(to Granier)* So Granier, What's the latest news? You spy on all these people as I've told you, I hope!

GRANIER: Yes, Mr. Jadin. Surely, Mr. Jadin. I have even surprised several times the new man making grimaces while looking at your office.

JADIN: Is that all?

GRANIER: No Mr. Jadin. In addition he pulled his tongue twice and thumbed his nose at you!

JADIN: Is that all?

GRANIER: No, Mr. Jadin. He also called me... *(hesitating)* a clot, Mr. Jadin!

JADIN: You? I couldn't care less about you! *(moves threateningly towards Granier)* I blame him for not using stronger insults. You may go,

	Granier! Keep me informed of whatever happens in this office. And I want to hear of serious things, do you understand?
GRANIER:	*(terribly scared)* I understand, Mr. Jadin. I am going out, Mr. Jadin. *(he leaves).*
JADIN:	*(to himself)* Next week I'm going to get rid of the new comer. When posted in the bush he'll know what it costs to kick against my wishes. Twenty months or more at a place where the temperature goes up to 50 degrees centigrade in the shade, will teach him a lesson. One cannot attack someone like Jadin and get away with it! Attacking a wolf like me. He will leave, tomorrow, not next week. And he called himself a lion! *(howling)* Granier! Granier!
GRANIER:	*(answering from afar)* Yes, Mr. Jadin. I'm coming, Mr. Jadin. At your service, Mr. Jadin.
JADIN:	*(still yelling)* I don't want to see any more of the new comer. He must leave tomorrow for his post in the bush! Take all necessary steps!
GRANIER:	*(coming in)* Yes, Mr. Jadin. At your service, Mr. Jadin. As you want it, Mr. Jadin... I am a fool Mr. Jadin... *(bows several times, Jadin takes huge puffs at his cigar, with his feet on the desk, while his slave fans him most vigorously).*

(and the curtain falls)

ACT III

(the curtain rises)

SCENE I

Action now takes place in Maiduguri, a forlorn place in the African bush, very far from the heart of the country. The temperature is extremely high. There are several commercial houses including OSCA and OLAF. The action takes place in the office of OSCA. The furniture is scanty. A large table on which four black employees are working is placed on the left, facing the stage. On the right is the door leading to the shop. Still on the right but nearer the stage is a little desk at which is seated a European. One can recognise the new man from Port Harcourt who is busy writing. Two cupboards, a safe and a stool are the remaining furniture in the room. A resident of the area comes in, carrying several pieces of cloth on his shoulders as well as enamel plates in his hands.

THE CUSTOMER: *A salamu Alaikum. (drops noisily everything on the table.)*

THE NEW MAN: *(with a start)* Good morning. What's it? *(low)* What does this one want? For the whole week that I have been here I have not seen a single soul. Could he be the first customer? *(aloud)* What do you want sir?

THE CUSTOMER: *(in broken English)* I want know price for cheap goods.

THE NEW MAN: *(aside)* Cheap goods! Isn't he exaggerating? Cheap goods *(aloud)* Yes, of course, just a moment, please. Sit down there. *(aside)* The very first customer! So I must handle him well. I don't want to behave like Jadin who treats everybody brutally and with insults. *(he consults his price lists)* It is 1,050 Frs. per piece of suiting material and 750 Frs. for a dozen of plates. I add 10% for transportation, 5% for other costs and handling charges, it increases the price by 25%, I'll round up the total and I'll wait for the fellow's reaction. It will always be easy to reduce prices later. *(to the customer)* It is 1,500 Frs. for a piece of suiting material and 1,100 Frs. for a dozen plates.

THE CUSTOMER: It's very dear!

THE NEW MAN: Dear!

THE CUSTOMER: Yes sir, Too dear! I go pay 1,100 and 750 Frs. only. Good price, sir.

THE NEW MAN: No, it's not good for me. It's a good price for you, perhaps, but not for me!

THE CUSTOMER: Sir, good price for white man!

THE NEW MAN: No way. It's perhaps a good price for blacks but not for whites.

THE CUSTOMER: True talk, commander! It's good for you, I swear!

THE NEW MAN: No way, man!

THE CUSTOMER: I pay you 1,200 and 800 Francs!

THE NEW MAN: No! It's too low!

Act III, Scene I

THE CUSTOMER: I swear, my general, that I am buying only to please you!

THE NEW MAN: I give them to you at 1,450 and 1,050 Frs. last price, just to please you!

THE CUSTOMER: No sir, 1,200 and 800!

THE NEW MAN: 1,450 and 1,050!

THE CUSTOMER: True, Doctor, 1,200 and 800, me lose on it. Me please you only. You are like my father. Me, small, small like your son. So you leave materials for 1,250 and plates 850 and you happy, me happy!

THE NEW MAN: 1,450 and 1,050, Not a kobo less!

THE CUSTOMER: My commandant, you too dear, me your little boy, so you do me pleasure.

THE NEW MAN: *(looking tired)* I give them to you for 1,400 and 1,000 Frs.

THE CUSTOMER: My father. You done forget, your little boy! Market price very very low! Nobody fit buy now, I want make only little profit, No more!

THE NEW MAN: *(aside)* Good heavens! I am successively commandant, general, boss, doctor and father! Why not captain in the navy or admiral? Well, there is scarcely any water here and this poor devil has never seen a boat in all his life! if all customers are like him, it's going to be interesting indeed.

(aloud) So, do you agree or not? 1,400 and 1,000 Frs!

THE CUSTOMER: My Colonel, I fit pay 1,300 and 900, No more palaver!

THE NEW MAN: Fine! Agreed! Bring the money, and let's settle the matter!

THE CUSTOMER: Right, my General! Thanks my General! I go fit bring money now now! (*goes out*) (*another local trader comes in, carrying on his shoulder a piece of suiting materials, and in the hand some enamel plates, just like the first customer*).

THE NEW MAN: (*aside*) Jesus! Another one! (*two other customers enter, followed by another one, then by six others, then by many more*).

THE NEW MAN: (*terrified by the sight of such a crowd*) What a nightmare! What a disaster! Having to bargain for a whole hour with this chap, and being called all kinds of names: Doctor, General, you name it... Ah no! We have had enough for today. Let's stop this invasion. (*talking to one of the clerks*) Simeon!

SIMEON: Sir.

THE NEW MAN: Lock the door. There are enough customers for today. (*The customers settle down, squatting, waiting for their turn... discussing aloud and spitting saliva on the floor.*) (*howling*) Silence. (*There is silence but it lasts just a few seconds. The noise is now louder than*

Act III, Scene II

before) (shrugging his shoulders) What kind of situation do I find myself in? If my mother could see me now! The good old lady would have a shock!

(the curtain falls)

ACT III

(the curtain rises)

SCENE II

(Same background, the new man is seated behind his desk. A lot of papers piled on it. He looks preoccupied. Someone knocks at the door)

THE NEW MAN: Come in. *(A European enters. He is about thirty years old. He has brown hair, a pleasant look and a very pronounced French accent. He moves towards the new man's desk.)*

THE VISITOR: So you are the new OSCA Director?

THE NEW MAN: Yes, I am! But my title is Manager...

THE VISITOR: Well, let me introduce myself! I am the Director of OLAF the other French commercial company operating in this town. Well, between you and me, Director and Manager are only names. What matters is to get our pay at the end of the month!

THE NEW MAN: *(beginning to laugh)* Ah, money! Always money! As for me, sir, I am working for the pleasure of it. But what is your name by the way?

The Last Slave Traders

THE VISITOR: Pitras, Marius Pitras.

THE NEW MAN: Marius?

PITRAS: Yes, it's my old man who gave me that silly name! Once one has it, it's for keeps! And you?

LAURENT: Laurent is my name, Pierre Laurent. How long have you been here?

PITRAS: Four years already.

LAURENT: You must be very familiar with the area!

PITRAS: Oh yes! But not to the extent of knowing this bunch of crooks! Likeable crooks, I must confess, but the devil knows how ravenous! Yes those chaps are very hungry and their appetite for money has no limit!

LAURENT: Is it always hot here?

PITRAS: Oh yes! No doubt about it. But the great heat will not begin till after fifteen days. It is then that you'll see temperatures running from 48 to 50 degrees centigrades in your office.

LAURENT: Fifty degrees! So how do you manage without electricity and hence without fans?

PITRAS: I manage, I have a pankah above me and a "Zebra" making it work very fast. When it's too hot, I have my barrel!

LAURENT: Your barrel?

Act III, Scene II

PITRAS: Yes my dear, a barrel! You'll see it working fully in fifteen days. I have it filled with fresh water every morning, and every day at 10 O'clock, when the heat begins, PLOUFF! I plunge into it.

LAURENT: *(astounded)* Really? In a barrel?

PITRAS: Nothing could be more true! A good empty barrel of 200 litres and I supervise operations from inside it!

LAURENT: *(aside)* Incredible! A barrel! Anyway I'll see. *(to Pitras)* And are you enjoying Maiduguri?

PITRAS: The hell I do! I live in clover! The important thing is to be organised. A panka, a barrel... to fight against the heat, a gun, a horse, a wife to fight against boredom. And we have 1,500 good kilometres of impossible roads which protect us from the nuisance of interference from the head office!

LAURENT: Are you married?

PITRAS: Married? Not at all! I live with a black girl, no doubt. I philander, too, no doubt, but that is all! A small time affair, that's what it is! Oh! I was forgetting, we have an extra master trump to defeat the people of the head office!

LAURENT: Really? What is it?

PITRAS: The heat, good heavens! For three months of the year, we have, as I've already said temperatures going up to 50 centigrades in the shade. During that time, you don't go out in the afternoon. The fools who did went back home in a coffin or almost. But we have peace, oh yes! total peace! In addition, as telephones hardly ever work, nobody tries to call us. The mail? Better not to talk about it. It is highly irregular, and the road to Maiduguri is cut three months during the rainy season! What could be better than that?

LAURENT: I see! It's a real cushy number! You've for yourself a nice little nest!

PITRAS: Yes, indeed! In fact, if you wish to follow my footsteps, I can give you a few tips. My wife can introduce you to one of her sisters. In matters of horses, I am an expert. OK. Bye bye! Come and see me whenever you want to.

LAURENT: Bye bye and thanks for your visit. *(Pitras goes out).*

LAURENT: *(aside)* By God! That man has original ideas! He is worth cultivating! His idea of the panka is far from stupid. That of the Barrel is cranky but perhaps effective. As for a "wife," I'll see about that later. The same for the horse, As for the gun... well when I have enough money I'll consider *(aloud)* Simeon!

SIMEON: Sir!

Act III, Scene II

LAURENT: Do you know a carpenter or somebody who can make me a panka?

SIMEON: Boss, you mean a panka?

LAURENT: Yes, a panka! The thing that blows air when pulled...

SIMEON: Oh yes, boss, I know... the white man of OLAF has got one!

LAURENT: Exactly! So go now now and find me a carpenter! I want a panka tomorrow, I must fight the heat right from now on!

SIMEON: OK boss, I'm going! *(Simeon goes out)*

LAURENT: *(aside)* First the panka, then the gun, followed by the horse and the wife. The only thing left would then be the barrel, but I can't imagine Jadin face to face with that object! *(laughs)* I can't imagine Jadin seeing his manager in a barrel full of water! But Jadin is far away. In any case to hell with him! What? Five O'clock? Let's close the bloody shop, we've had enough business for today. *(to the clerks)* Close and go, you fellows, and good night! *(aside)* Yes, Jadin is far away, 1,500km from here and 1,500kms of bad roads! How right is Pitras; And now let us think about serious matters! First my cup of tea, then a game of tennis... *(to a clerk)* Hurry up man! It's time to go!

(they go out and the curtain falls)

ACT III

(the curtain rises)

SCENE III

The stage is divided into two. On one side we recognise Jadin's office, on the other is the office of the new man. Jadin is seated at his desk, the new man at his, with his head covered with bandages.

LAURENT:	Simeon!
SIMEON:	Yes, boss!
LAURENT:	Ring OSCA Port Harcourt and ask for Jadin.
SIMEON:	Yes, boss, *(rings the exchange and asks for 4634, the number of OSCA Port Harcourt.) (to Laurent)* He says he is going to try, sir, but the line is bad.
LAURENT:	I'm not surprised, it is always bad!
JADIN:	*(talking to himself, 1,500kms away)* I wonder what this little clot of a new man is doing. I am worried to have him so far away from me without anybody to supervise him.
LAURENT:	*(aside)* I got away with it. I was lucky! Two somersaults in this damned car! Some wounds on the head, multiple bruises, but nothing really serious. It's not like the poor driver who's got multiple fractures. So strange, these accidents, brakes that give away and off you go! You may even die in the process! *(The telephone rings at the same time*

Act III, Scene III

both in Jadin's and in Laurent's offices. Jadin takes the receiver, pulls a sour face, and Simeon goes to the telephone and takes the receiver.)

SIMEON: Yes, Mr. Jadin. Yes sir, he's in.

LAURENT: Is it Port Harcourt?

SIMEON: Yes sir... yes, boss!

LAURENT: *(seizing the receiver from Simeon's hands)* Is it Mr. Jadin?

JADIN: *(pulling a face more and more sour)* Yes, this is Mr. Jadin, *(shouting)* What do you want? I hope that you are calling me about a serious matter. I will not accept big telephone bills!

LAURENT: *(also yelling because the line is bad)* It is to inform you that....

JADIN: *(howling)* Talk louder! I can't hear a word! *(to himself)* What does he want again? Why did I say again, since he has never asked for anything? But I maintain the word AGAIN because this time it is once too much!

LAURENT: It is to inform you that I have had an accident...

JADIN: *(aloud)* An accident? *(to himself)* What right had he to have an accident?

LAURENT: Yes an accident!

JADIN: *(to himself)* Bastard! One month there and already an accident! *(on the telephone)* You know, I do hope, that the company is not responsible for accidents occurring after office hours... and that accidents resulting from hunting and sports are not covered!

LAURENT: But Mr. Jadin...

JADIN: *(to himself)* You little clot! *(on the telephone)* You better know that I don't like accidents. I sack those who have accidents! *(to himself)* Especially those who are not recommended by Paris. To think that by mistake I thought he was recommended by Paris! My God! A case of mistaken identity! He should have taken the first boat like the others!

LAURENT: But Mr. Jadin... *(low)* When is he going to allow me to talk? Uncouth fellow! Rowdy character, stupid ass!

JADIN: *(to himself)* By the way, what kind of accident is it? I hope it's not a motor accident, a brand new car! *(on the telephone, howling even louder)* What kind of accident did you have?

LAURENT: The delivery van Mr. Jadin...

JADIN: *(to himself roaring)* Son of a bitch! A brand new van. *(on the telephone)* With the brand new van? Aren't you crazy? A vechicle just out of the assembly plant!

LAURENT: The driver has a broken leg...

JADIN: What about the van? Any damage?

LAURENT: The right arm broken in two places.

Act III, Scene III

JADIN: *(to himself)* To hell with the driver. Tell me about the van! *(on the telephone)* What about the van?

LAURENT: And several wounds everywhere on the body.

JADIN: And the van?

LAURENT: And on his face...

JADIN: *(on the telephone)* Talk about the van please. *(to himself)* I am furious! To hell with the driver!

LAURENT: *(to himself)* To hell with his van! *(on the telephone)* As far as I'm concerned....

JADIN: *(red of anger)* The van, for Christ sake!

LAURENT: I have light wounds and bruises all over my body. Nothing serious! *(to himself)* When will he stop talking about his bloody van? This man is a lunatic!

JADIN: *(to himself)* What impudence to talk about himself now. *(on the telephone)* What about the van! Do you hear me? Christ Almighty!

LAURENT: I shall be obliged to stay away from the office for several days...

JADIN: And the van? *(suddenly realising)* What! absenting yourself for several days from office?

LAURENT: Yes sir, on the doctor's advice!

JADIN: To hell with that quack! I order you, me,

	Jadin, to attend office... your condition is more than satisfactory. In fact you need to put in some extra hours.
LAURENT:	I beg your pardon! *(to himself)* You have got a fat chance, poor chap!
JADIN:	A few extra hours will do you good! What about the van? Do you hear me? *(spacing out the syllables)* The de-li-very van!
LAURENT:	*(to himself)* Damn his van as well as himself. There's nothing in his head but his bloody van! *(on the telephone)* Badly damaged!
JADIN:	What! A van worth a million francs!
LAURENT:	*(who can hardly hold back a laugh)* It's become a heap of junk, sir!
JADIN:	Can you repeat?
LAURENT:	*(laughing)* It's become a pile of useless scrap iron sir!
JADIN:	And you find that funny
LAURENT:	Very funny indeed! You make me laugh! It's a miracle that the driver and I are alive, but you are only interested in your van.
JADIN:	*(to himself)* But does he realise I don't bloody care about his little self and the driver? Their commercial value is nil, whereas the van appears in my books for the sum of 1,167,000 Francs. *(on the telephone)* And you were driving of course!

Act III, Scene III

LAURENT: No! The driver was!

JADIN: You'll have to prove it! Otherwise, for such a serious lapse, it's the first boat! You realise what it means to write off a new vehicle? *(Enter Granier. He stands near Jadin's desk but the latter doesn't notice him).*

LAURENT: Yes, Mr. Jadin. *(to himself)* Does he realise I couldn't care less for him, his big belly and his van? My life before everything else, he should know!

JADIN: What did you say?

LAURENT: Nothing, Mr. Jadin.

JADIN: I thought I heard you say something.

LAURENT: I said nothing, Mr. Jadin.

JADIN: So is it well understood? I need the evidence that you were not driving. Your future in this company depends on that.

LAURENT: *(to himself)* What future? He must be joking! *(on the telephone)* Yes, Mr. Jadin.

GRANIER: *(grinning rather stupidly)* Yes Mr. Jadin, yes, Mr. Jadin.

JADIN: *(noticing Granier's presence) (to himself)* But what is this idiot doing here? *(on the telephone)* Expect my visit one of these days...

LAURENT: Which day, Mr. Jadin?

JADIN: *(to himself)* Which day? What does he think?

	When in fact I want to surprise him. *(on the telephone)* Very soon, in a month or two!
LAURENT:	*(to himself)* One could not be more precise! Bastard! *(on the telephone)* Very well, sir.
JADIN:	OK. Bye bye! Ah by the way since you have not been able to maintain your van, you'll have to hire a bicycle.
LAURENT:	*(to himself)* What does he think? *(on the telephone)* Yes, Mr. Jadin... Certainly, Mr. Jadin!
JADIN:	And do not leave your office even for a minute!
LAURENT:	*(to himself and giving Jadin a V sign)* Get lost! *(on the telephone)* But certainly, Mr. Jadin!
JADIN:	I know these quacks! They all exaggerate. They present a simple scratch as a serious wound.
LAURENT:	*(to himself)* Enough is enough. Come off it!
JADIN:	And a sprain into a broken leg!
LAURENT:	Yes, Mr. Jadin.
JADIN:	You better know there's only one person in command here, and it's me, not the bloody Doctor! *(to himself)* These doctors! What a bloody set! *(on the telephone)* I'll see you soon, keep the bicycle in good condition. You must look well after the equipment!
LAURENT:	Yes, Mr. Jadin. Good-bye, Mr. Jadin. *(ges-*

Act III, Scene IV

ticulating wildly and making signs to show he cares the least about Jadin's recommendations) Bye-bye Mr. Jadin!

GRANIER: *(bowing behind Jadin)* Yes, Mr. Jadin. Goodbye, Mr. Jadin... At your service Mr. Jadin.

(the curtain falls)

ACT III

(the curtain rises)

SCENE IV

Maiduguri office. The panka is fixed in the middle of the ceiling. A young black boy seated on the ground is pulling it to and fro at full speed. Laurent at his desk. The two black employees seated behind the large table. Laurent goes to the calendar and tears out a leaf.

LAURENT: It's a month since Jadin advised me of his visit. He should be coming any time from now. *(to Simeon)* Simeon, is everything in order?

SIMEON: Yes, boss, everything.

LAURENT: Is the file up-to-date? And the books?

SIMEON: Yes, sir!

LAURENT: You know that the Port Harcourt General Manager is to inspect us anytime from now?

SIMEON: *(with fear and respect)* The big Port Harcourt Manager?

LAURENT:	Yes, the big Manager! *(to himself)* The big bastard yes! A manager, no! He doesn't have the makings of a general manager *(he goes back to his seat)*. *(Loud noise outside, and suddenly Jadin appears, walking hurriedly. He trips up in a table and pays it back with a hefty kick.)*
JADIN:	Accursed table! Accursed country! *(Laurent stands up and stretches his hand to Jadin who has come near him. Jadin ignores the outstretched hand. Laurent keeps his hand hanging in the air, and looks at it. Slowly, he brings it down.)*
JADIN:	*(to himself)* To hell with his hand!
LAURENT:	*(to himself)* He despises my hand, my God!
JADIN:	*(to himself)* The hand of a thief, the hand of a scoundrel!
LAURENT:	*(to himself)* Leaving my hand in the air like that! He will pay for it!
JADIN:	It's awfully hot in your place! And so much sand!
LAURENT:	As for heat and sand we have a lot of them!
JADIN:	*(suddenly realising the presence of the pankah)* What's this gadget? Are you mad? A pankah! Have it removed immediately! It looks too colonialist. A bad reminder of slavery! You have the nerve to have it installed without my permission?
LAURENT:	But there's no fan, sir, and it's very hot!

Act III, Scene IV

JADIN: Shut up!

LAURENT: Besides, I paid for it with my own money!

JADIN: That's the last straw! It would have been the limit had you debited the company for the cost of a pankah! Your station does not make enough profits for us to give you a fan. In two years, perhaps, if the business improves...

LAURENT: Fine, sir!

JADIN: Now, do you understand? Get that thing removed! *(he points at the pankah)*

LAURENT: Yes, sir,

JADIN: *(noticing that Laurent has a boil on his arm)* Tell me, what have you got on your arm?

LAURENT: Please, sir?

JADIN: *(with air of disgust)* But it's leprosy! That's the last straw! I'll have to give you a bell to let people know you are around for them to part to let you through.

LAURENT: It's a boil Mr. Jadin which I got buying your hides and skins!

JADIN: Shut up. It's leprosy I am telling you!

LAURENT: All right, all right since you insist!

JADIN: Shut up you jerk!

LAURENT: Yes, sir!

The Last Slave Traders

JADIN: And now, show me your books, and be quick about it!

LAURENT: Here they are, sir! *(pushes an armful of books to Jadin who sits at the desk.)*

JADIN: *(looking through the books)* They are badly kept. Here for example. You will have to open this book all over again. *(throws down the books at a corner of the office.)* The same observation goes for this one, and that one *(he throws them to the other corner).* You know what? I'm not at all satisfied. The destruction of the van, the pankah, and now the negligence in your duties! Your fate is in the balance! Obstinate as you are and giving the impression that you don't care about anybody!

LAURENT: Yes, sir, no, sir.

JADIN: Never forget this. Whether in the sticky mud of Opobo and Port Harcourt or in the burning sands of Maiduguri, I am still the boss! Do you hear me?

LAURENT: *(to himself)* Congratulations. What a beautiful speech! The only thing missing is the national anthem! *(to Jadin)* Yes, sir.

JADIN: *(continuing to flip through the files and books)* Results are nothing to boast about. You're the least profit-making branch of the Company.

LAURENT: But sir!

Act III, Scene IV

JADIN: There's no "but"! I am only interested in results, remember that!

LAURENT: *(to himself)* But this branch was opened only a few months ago, eh! How can he expect such rapid results? *(to Jadin)* OK., sir.

JADIN: I expect a rapid and substantial improvement.

LAURENT: *(to himself)* I've already heard that somewhere. *(to Jadin)* Yes, sir.

JADIN: You have nothing else to say?

LAURENT: Yes, sir, It's about my accommodation.

JADIN: Your accommodation?

LAURENT: Yes. You know that I'm living in a bungalow rented from the administration.

JADIN: *(surprised)* Ah, I hear this for the first time.

LADURENT: And now the administration wants it back.

JADIN: So?

LAURENT: And so, in a month, I'll find myself without accommodation!

JADIN: Just that? Manage, my friend!

LAURENT: Manage what?

JADIN: *(angrily)* Yes, manage, and don't talk to me again about that. Live in your shop, in your office, wherever you please, I don't care! Look, get a mud hut built. I allocate 30,000

	francs for the purpose, not a kobo more.
LAURENT:	A mud hut?
JADIN:	Yes, a mud hut! and 30,000 francs, not a kobo more. Now let's talk about more serious things. You think too much about yourself, my friend, too much about your little comforts. Think a bit more about OSCA, and not about the house you live in. OSCA is your mother! Realise that!
LAURENT:	*(to himself)* An unnatural mother, yes!
JADIN:	So put all these books in order. OK? Now I would like to see our competitors. Who are they?
LAURENT:	*(speaking off)* A mud hut! Bloody hell! He goes too far! I have no desire to play either Robinson Crusoe or the savages! And 30,000 francs! When he lives in a 30,000,000 francs bungalow! Three more zeros to the right!
JADIN:	Answer me. What about the competitors?
LAURENT:	*(lost in his thoughts)* He dares to say: This company is your mother. This company is your mother! This company is your mother! Bloody bastard, I can produce such a mother every day.
JADIN:	He must be day-dreaming, my God! *(goes near Laurent and hits him on the shoulder)*
LAURENT:	*(with a start)* Sir!

Act III, Scene IV

JADIN: You are day-dreaming, my friend! You need to be shaken up a bit. I would like to see our competitors. What are they?

LAURENT: *(reciting)* UAC, HOLT, PZ, LEVENTIS, THE FRENCH COMPANY...and LONDON and KANO. Ah I was forgetting WESTERN SUDAN. *(to himself)* 30,000 francs. What a shame! This company my mother? A scoundrel of a woman, yes!

JADIN: We'll first visit the French Company. It's the fiercest competitor we have.

LAURENT: Oh yes, you are right! *(to himself)* 30,000 francs. What can one do with such a ridiculous amount? Sleep under bridges? There are no bridges around here! In a haystack? Not a single blade of grass grows here! A little zero will have to be added to the end, to the end of the 30,000 francs...

JADIN: Yes, watch these people. They have a grudge against our company!

LAURENT: *(to himself)* A grudge against our mother? That bitch! *(aloud)* Really!

JADIN: I therefore order you not to have any relationship with that lot! No question of inviting them home.

LAURENT: *(to himself)* Which home? Worth no more than 30,000 francs?

JADIN: Nor to accept their invitations that have only

	one aim, to worm information out of your!
LAURENT:	*(still thinking about the same thing)* One question, sir. Was it 30,000 francs. that you said a short while ago?
JADIN:	What 30,000 francs?
LAURENT:	For building the...
JADIN:	*(cutting him short)* Don't bring up that topic again! Of course it's 30,000 francs, not a kobo more. Ah shit! It's a bit too late to go and see the competitors! I'll continue to check your books till mid-day and at two we'll go and see those bastards, starting with those sharks of the French Company! *(He sits down and checks the books on his desk. When he has finished he throws them on the floor.)* Good heavens! It's lamentable! More than ever. Your fate hangs in the balance!
LAURENT:	*(to himself)* Why doesn't he cut this bloody affair once for all? I've had enough of his bragging! The 30,000 francs, the bitch of a mother, the mud hut, and now the ban on seeing people! Well, I'll take a walk outside. *(he goes out)*
JADIN:	*(continuing to throw the books without raising his head)* Yes my friend! It hangs by a thread! Your future in our reputable company has been seriously jeopardized *(raising his head)*. But where is he? Ah, that's too much. I'm shouting like mad and the fucker has disappeared! *(to a clerk)* Call the son of a bitch!

Act III, Scene IV

SIMEON: *(shocked)* Who, sir?

JADIN: That runt! *(pointing at Laurent's desk)* Ask him to come back immediately!

SIMEON: *(rushing out)* My boss a son of a bitch?

JADIN: *(to himself)* That's the last straw! Letting me to shout myself hoarse while he clears out without saying a word! I'll put him on the first boat, there's no doubt about that. Now I have good grounds for doing it: Delivery van, pankah, books badly kept and now desertion of his post!

LAURENT: *(just coming)* Are you calling me, sir?

JADIN: Am I calling you? Good God, you couldn't be more right! You're to stay put as long as I m here. Sit down and see your errors! Some lines are badly drawn, some headings badly done, here black instead of red ink, in short an endless string of errors!

LAURENT: A few trifles sir! which do not prevent business from thriving, nor stop the earth from gyrating, nor myself from sleeping soundly, sir!

JADIN: *(yelling)* Insolent! Clot! Bastard. There are serious errors I am telling you. These could hinder the progress of our company, OSCA, the mother of us all, and seriously harm your career!

LAURENT: (to himself) My career! My career! Let us talk about it! Poor man!

JADIN: (to himself) Poor chap! unaware of the danger...

LAURENT: (to himself) Poor man!

JADIN: (to himself) Poor bastard!

LAURENT: (smiling) Poor chap!

JADIN: (a bad grimace on the lips) Poor man! (the clock strikes mid-day) (getting up) Fine. I'll see you soon!

LAURENT: (getting up too) I'll see you soon, sir.

(They go out of the office, followed by the clerks. The curtain falls).

ACT III

(the curtain rises)

SCENE V

The shop at OLAF, the other French Company. A wooden counter goes from one end of the wall to the other. Coarse shelves and a barrel are seen behind the counter. There's no one in the shop except a young black boy who is fanning himself and Jadin and Laurent who have just come in.

JADIN: (having looked around) These rogues are well established! I repeat and insist that you mustn't be friends with them!

Act III, Scene V

LAURENT: But sir, there are only two Frenchmen here, he and I. So...

JADIN: That's enough! My order is not to be questioned or discussed.

LAURENT: Yes, sir. *(aside)* The bastard must be joking!

JADIN: *(Seeing the barrel)* What's the use of that barrel?

LAURENT: The barrel? *(pretending to be surprised)* Which barrel?

JADIN: Don't you see the barrel over there?

LAURENT: Oh, that barrel? Oh yes, I see it sir! It must be used as... Well to be frank, I don't know sir, *(trying to divert his attention)* If you like, sir, we can go and visit UAC, another very active competitor...

JADIN: No, it's enough for to-day. I must see the agent of this company.

LAURENT: *(doing all he can to make Jadin leave)* He may have gone to town, or to a bush outlet. We could come back later on or tomorrow morning...

JADIN: It's all right! Let's wait here. *(enter Pitras wearing only bathing trunks).*

PITRAS: *(aloud)* Good day, sirs. To what do I owe the pleasure of your visit? *(to himself)* Pleasure? my foot!

JADIN: *(to himself)* Am I dreaming? This boy wears

only briefs! How is it possible?

PITRAS: *(jumping into the barrel, producing a loud noise of splashed water)* A minute please, let me sit on my throne.

JADIN: *(aside)* I must be dreaming for sure! *(a drop of water lands on his left eye)* No, I'm not dreaming! *(rubbing his eye)* This drop of water does exist, there is no doubt about it!

PITRAS: *(to Jadin)* My name is Pitras. I realise you are surprised, sir, but it's the most effective way to fight the inhuman heat. Look at yourself! You are sweating, feeling uncomfortable, undergoing suffering, while I am as happy as one can be.

JADIN: *(wiping his forehead) (aloud)* Yes, eh! eh! it's very original. *(aside)* I'm going to make a report about him. When his management in Port-Harcourt gets to know that their agent manages their business while sitting in a barrel, they will come down to earth! They will surely sack him, and replace him by an inexperienced agent and we shall benefit from that! We'll be the kings of the trade! *(aloud)* An excellent way indeed of fighting heat!

PITRAS: I have no fan, and I'm not satisfied with the pankah, so I had to find something else! *(A customer enters and asks the sales boy for something. The latter receives the money and brings it to Pitras, who takes it, counts it and throws the*

Act III, Scene V

	coins and notes into the drawer nearby) Heat makes you ingenious, you see? *(looking at Laurent)* When are you going to buy yourself a barrel, colleague?
LAURENT:	*(an ironical smile on his lips)* I've no idea. You better ask Mr. Jadin, my Managing Director.
JADIN:	*(who stiffens and makes a terrible grimace)* As a matter of fact, it's very original. I'll think about it. *(aside)* Me, to buy a barrel? Morons all of them!
PITRAS:	*(in an ironical tone)* But Mr. General Manager, others have solved the problem of heat in a different way. Some do it by spending the entire afternoon in their bath-tub filled with cold water. My method has the advantage of enabling me to work or at least be present. It's not easy to work in such extreme heat. *(leans out of the barrel and takes the thermometer from the counter.)* Do you realise? 48 degrees centigrade!
JADIN:	*(wiping his forehead and grimacing)* Yes, I can see.
PITRAS:	But the crankiest idea is that of a man from Brittany, who, dreaming of sea water, used one of his petrol stores as a swimming pool and poured a few bags of salt into the water to complete the illusion.
JADIN:	Hmm, humm. Yes. Quite ludicrous this idea!
PITRAS:	Oh you know in the bush! Moreover the

	breakages and wastage account is there to be used!
JADIN:	*(on the verge of a fit of hysteria) (to himself)* Breakages and wastage! Breakages and wastage! This guy must be an anarchist! *(aloud) (to Laurent)* Let's go, let's leave this place!
LAURENT:	Yes, sir.
PITRAS:	Bye bye, sirs. By the way, colleague, let me know if you need an empty barrel. I have a good one that I have just debited to breakages and wastage account. Ah! Come to my place on Sunday noon. We can have lunch together!
LAURENT:	But I... don't know....
PITRAS:	Please don't make such a fun! I shall depend on your coming, Good bye sirs.
JADIN:	Bye bye. *(Pitras stretches his hand. Jadin gets a few drops of water on the nose. He wipes his face)* *(aside)* Anarchist. He'll soon be sorry for what he has said! A nasty report about him will do him a lot of good. But wait, as I see him now, it may be better if he stays here. He doesn't look clever and he takes things easy. He cannot be so crafty, otherwise he wouldn''t make such remarks before me, the Managing Director of OSCA! Yes, after all it's better if he stays in Maiduguri. Those fools are capable of sending a good and capable fellow who will capture the entire market. No, no

	report! He can stay in his barrel all his life! *(aloud)* Bye bye Mr. Pitras. *(Jadin goes out backwards and looks at Pitras who waves to him.) (aloud)* Bye bye. Bye bye Mr. Pitras *(aloud)*. Fantastic! Incredible! *(both of them go out)*
PITRAS:	*(left alone)* Whoever he is, I don't care! Big or small, it's all the same! As far as I'm concerned, all men are equal! And the heat is the same for everybody. Equality in the heat! Let's go and have a drink! *(to the young salesman)* Hey my friend!
SALESMAN:	Yes, sir!
PITRAS:	I'm going home for ten minutes.
SALESMAN:	Yes, sir!
PITRAS:	*(coming out of his barrel, the water dripping down his body)* Oh! what one has to do to make a living! *(he goes out of the shop and the curtain falls).*

ACT III

(the curtain rises)

SCENE VI

The office of OSCA. Jadin is discussing with Laurent when the curtain rises. The ground is still littered with files and books.

JADIN:	This Pitras is a case, isn't he!
LAURENT:	Oh yes, sir!

JADIN:	I was amused by his barrel! I hope that you are not having one!
LAURENT:	*(aloud)* Oh no, Mr. Jadin. *(aside)* Not yet!
JADIN:	Or you'll leave by the first boat!
LAURENT:	Yes, sir!
JADIN:	It's incredible! A barrel inside a shop, with a white man in it! I've never seen such a thing during my forty years on the coast!
LAURENT:	But Mr. Jadin, here we are in Maiduguri, very near the Sahara! So the heat waves, the burning sands... Some people can't stand it!
JADIN:	You, the newly-arrived, I don't need your comments! But you'll have no barrel, I hope.
LAURENT:	*(aloud)* No, no, Mr. Jadin, *(aside)* not yet.
JADIN:	Nor a swimming pool filled with sea-water!
LAURENT:	*(aloud)* No, Mr. Jadin... *(aside)* I wish I had one!
JADIN:	Are you sure?
LAURENT:	Very sure, Mr. Jadin.
SPIRIT OF GRANIER:	*(floating in very loose clothes with large sleeves)* No, Mr. Jadin! At your service, Mr. Jadin!
JADIN:	*(who turns round but sees nothing)* No bath-tub with cold water?

Act III, Scene VI

LAURENT: No, Mr. Jadin.

SPIRIT OF GRANIER: *(louder still)* No, Mr. Jadin! No, Mr. Jadin.

JADIN: *(aside and turning round)* I thought I could hear the voice of Granier. *(aloud)* And the breakages and wastage account! Is it to be used or not?

LAURENT: Yes, Mr. Jadin. Eh... made to be used Mr. Jadin. Eh... not to be used Mr. Jadin!

SPIRIT OF GRANIER: Yes, Mr. Jadin. At your service, Mr. Jadin.

JADIN: *(looking around and seeing nothing) (aside)* By God! I must be ill! It must be the heat. *(aloud)* I repeat that you must not visit that Pitras man and I am telling you that... you will not get any vehicle for a long time... I am allocating to you, graciously, 30,000 francs to build a mud house, so that you know where to go when the administration summons you to vacate their building.

LAURENT: Yes, Mr. Jadin! *(aside)* You'll be lucky!

THE SPIRIT OF GRANIER: *(bowing)* Yes, Mr. Jadin! At your service, Mr. Jadin!

JADIN: *(ill at ease, and glacing around) (aside)* I am going to become mad if I remain a day longer in this bloody bush town. *(aloud)* The administration has been really good to have left you here for so long a time! And remember I want profits! Think of your mother, OSCA and of me, your father.

LAURENT: *(aloud)* Yes, sir!

SPIRIT OF GRANIER: *(curtsying)* Yes, Mr. Jadin. At your service, Mr. Jadin, I am a twerp, Mr. Jadin!

JADIN: *(aside)* These voices again! Blimey! I must leave this bloody place in a rush! Or I'll go stark mad! A few days more here and I'll do like Pitras, I'll be in a barrel. *(aloud)* Especially don't forget that whether in the muds of Opobo or in the sands of Maiduguri, I remain the only boss! *(sound of military music sounding like the Marseillaise, the French national anthem)*

SPIRIT OF GRANIER: Congratulations, Mr. Jadin, you spoke very well, Mr. Jadin!

LAURENT: Yes, Mr. Jadin.

SPIRIT OF GRANIER: *(several curtsies)* Yes, Mr. Jadin, At your service, Mr. Jadin.

JADIN: *(aside)* Always these bloody voices! And now it seems to me that I see Granier... here, close by... *(tries to seize him but the spirit escapes)* *(aloud)* Well, Bye bye!

LAURENT: *(stretching his hand, and immediately dropping it)* *(aloud)* Good bye, sir and safe journey. *(aside)* Bastard! You can go to hell!

Act III, Scene VI

JADIN: *(from the door step)* Good bye. And don't forget that your fate hangs in the balance. If you make the slightest mistake, it will be the first boat!

SPIRIT OF GRANIER: *(curtsying even harder)* Yes, Mr. Jadin. You are right, Mr. Jadin. I'm a fool, Mr. Jadin... *(the door closes on Jadin. The spirit of Granier has just enough time to go through)*

LAURENT: *(aside)* May the devil kill you by inches or take you on board! Now let's deal with serious matters. *(calling Simeon)* Simeon! Simeon!

SIMEON: Yes, boss!

LAURENT: Is everything ready?

SIMEON: Yes, sir!

LAURENT: Ok! Let's operate them and straight away! *(two pankahs, one just unfurled, are set in motion frantically by two young black boys. A huge barrel is introduced on the stage...)* Simeon!

SIMEON: Yes, Oga sah!

LAURENT: Debit breakages and wastage account with one carton of beer, 12 tins of milk, 3 bottles of champagne, 4....

(and the curtain falls)

ACT IV

(the curtain rises)

The action takes place twenty years later. Jadin's office is the same, same disposal, same little window enabling the Director to see the main office. Laurent is easily recognisable. He has put on weight. Laurent, THE NEW MAN man at the beginning of the play is now Managing Director of OSCA in place of Jadin.) (Laurent stands in front of a huge safe, whose door faces the stage. There is another safe, beside the first, but considerably smaller. Both are full of bags of money. More bags of money on the floor.

LAURENT: *(alone)* One, two, three. One for them, two for me! *(he puts two bags into the big safe and one into the smaller one)* Four, five, six. One for them, two for me! *(same acting as above)* Six, seven, eight. Nothing for them. All for me! *(puts the three bags in the huge safe and continues to throw the bags in the required direction, animated by a great joy) (stopping for a moment)* It took me a long time to understand, but at last I got the point! No pity for these big companies! They are rolling in money and they have no pity for anybody, let us take the case of Jadin. Their henchman for so long a time, his company, OSCA, to call it by its name, his mother as he used to say, threw him out as soon as he fell ill! Kicked out like a poor bastard! He deserved it as a person, no doubt, but not as an employee! Poor Jadin! As it is, in such an environment, it isn't easy being oneself. As for me, I must be far different from the newly arrived man I was twenty

Act IV

years ago. I am now a heartless slave trader, like Jadin himself!

Ah, money! Dear money! *(caresses the bags in the big safe)* All that is mine, I've lost count of what I have in France in cash and assets! Ah my little ones! *(caressing the bags)* My dear little ones, I love you! You are my children! Who else do I have apart from you? *(remains silent for a while and walks up and down).* There was this war and I remained here while some unfortunate ones went and got killed. Poor chaps! Idiots, as Jadin used to say. I would rather call them unfortunate ones, that's all. I made a little fortune. I filled bags like these. It's funny how money brings money. It snowballs! Then I threw my good intentions overboard. Gradually I became a slave trader like the others.

In every man indeed there is a dormant slave dealer! This dirty money that I love so much has taken possession of my heart, and I can't count anymore the number of times I behaved badly! If today I rob the company, it's perfectly normal, it is how things are linked! *(collects some bags from the floor and throws them into the safes)* One, two, three. One for them, two for me! But is it robbery? No, it's, hatred! One, two, three, nothing for them, all for me! A great hatred against them to please myself! An incommensurable hatred that I scarcely gauge.

One, two, three, two for them, one for me. Oh no! One for them, two for me! *(removes a bag from the smaller safe and throws it into the bigger one)* I hate them for what they've done to me, Jadin and the others. They made a robot out of me, a robot distributing kicks here and there, into black and white buttocks, kicks, both moral and physical! *(somebody knocks at the door)*

LAURENT: Just a minute. *(quickly shuts the two safes)* Come in! *(enters a man, Granier's carbon copy, having the same stupid and stupefied look)* Blimey! What else do you want?

GRANIER JUNIOR: Yes, Mr. Laurent. At your service, Mr. Laurent. Nothing, Mr. Laurent!

LAURENT: Oh you! I have seen enough of your bloody face! You are but a copy of your father, only worse!

GRANIER JUNIOR: Yes, Mr. Laurent. At your service, Mr. Laurent, I am a fool, Mr. Laurent!

LAURENT: I like to hear you say it.

GRANIER JUNIOR: Yes, Mr. Laurent!

LAURENT: What do you want? You are getting on my nerves!

GRANIER JUNIOR: It's about the new man, Mr. Laurent!

LAURENT: What about him?

GRANIER JUNIOR: He does not show any respect to me. Mr.

Act IV

> Laurent. *(looks sad and pulls a handkerchief from his pocket)*

LAURENT: Really, Granier?

GRANIER JUNIOR: Yes, Mr. Laurent. He called me... an old fossil, Mr. Laurent. *(wipes his right eye)*

GRANIER JUNIOR: Yes, Mr. Laurent. He called me... an old

LAURENT: *(aside)* He's bloody right! *(aloud)* Oh really? *(aside)* He will make his way in life, the dear young fellow!

GRANIER JUNIOR: So Mr. Laurent *(he begins to sniffle)* after ten years with the company you know, it is rather painful....

LAURENT: *(aside)* He'll probably go very high, just like me.

GRANIER JUNIOR: That's not all, Mr. Laurent. The bachelors made a lot of noise last night! Again they played football on the verandah.

LAURENT: Ah those dirty swines! Call them for me! They will see what stuff I'm made of! It will be the first boat for them, Oh no. Rather the first plane! *(aside)* One must move with the times.

GRANIER JUNIOR: As for the blacks, Mr. Laurent, they do not show any respect to me either...

LAURENT: *(aside)* I understand them, with such a face what can he expect? *(aloud)* It's the sign of the times, my poor fellow! The last world war has turned everything upside down. A wind of independence, of madness, is blowing over the world. So you must know the ropes! Anyway, tell all the whites and all the blacks to come to my office. These gentlemen cannot stand any more discrimination, so they say, well I do not discriminate when I sack, I sack both blacks and whites!

GRANIER JUNIOR: Yes, Mr. Laurent. At your service, Mr. Laurent. *(he goes out).*

LAURENT: I wonder what I'm going to tell them. Whatever I say or do reminds me of Jadin. Sometimes I seem to be hearing and seeing him. As if the words coming from my mouth were coming out of his. *(walks up and down the office)* I wonder what I'm going to tell them! I no longer believe in what I say or do! My mouth doesn't utter the words of my heart. First boat, first plane, it's enough of that! Enough! Giving kicks and insults! To hell with all that! Money can corrode like an acid. I am fed up to put on an act! I wish to be myself again! I will tell both blacks and whites that I'm leaving them, that I repudiate all I've been... *(continues to walk up and down without a word and without seeing the black and white employees entering one after the other. They seem stupefied. Granier junior is the last to enter. He shuts the door behind).*

GRANIER JUNIOR: Here you are, Mr. Laurent. They are all here, all without exception, the blacks and

Act IV

the whites!

LAURENT: Gentlemen, I sent for you all *(they look surprised, not used to being addressed as gentlemen)* to let you know something important. *(They look dismayed, shake their heads, and converse in a low tone)* I'm not going to threaten you to put you on the first boat or plane this time, for I am the one to do so for a change. I have decided to call it quits with OSCA, Africa and all my life here.

I'm going to start all over again in a new environment. Before going I'll ask you not to act like me. Behave like human beings, not like slave traders. Life is short. Don't poison your own life, don't poison the life of others. Before going I'll give you all I possess. But please, be wise, behave, don't fight one another for this blasted money! *(joy replaces fear and dismay on all the faces) (Laurent opens the two safes, takes the bags and throws them one after the other, behind him. The blacks and the whites pounce on them and struggle to collect as much as they can. It's free for all. There's confusion, torn money bags, kicks, blows, curses, bank notes, coins flying and rolling in all directions)*

(looking on) I told them to be wise, to behave, and they are all fighting, both blacks and whites. Before money, colour doesn't count! I told them: don't do what I did, and look at what they are doing! Miserable little men, seeds of potential slave dealers! I abandon

you all to your dire fate!

(The fight goes on, frantically, some are left unconscious on the floor, others are on their knees, or on their stomachs, crawling towards the bags of money. Granier Junior participates in the brawl) Here! Have more of it! *(he throws more bags)* More wood for your fire, my poor fellows. *(he opens and pours the last sack)* As for myself, I am off globe trotting. I want to see all the world before leaving it. After all we only live once. *(he opens the door and looks a last time at the fight going on)* Poor chaps! slave traders, all of you, both blacks and whites!

GRANIER JUNIOR: *(arriving completely dishevelled, with a black eye and torn clothes)* Mr. Laurent! Don't leave me, take me with you! Mr. Laurent, please!

LAURENT: No, stay here with them. There's no place for you where I'm going. My post here is vacant. Take it if you so wish.

GRANIER JUNIOR: Mr. Laurent, is that true?

LAURENT: Take my seat. I am telling you! *(aside)* Stupid as he is, he will do less harm than any other person! *(he goes out)*.

GRANIER JUNIOR: *(curtsies)* Mr. Laurent! At your service! Mr. Laurent, I'm a clot! Mr. Laurent...

(And The Curtain Falls)

THE END

www.ingramcontent.com/pod-product-compliance
Lightning Source LLC
Chambersburg PA
CBHW071224160426
43196CB00012B/2412